Praise for

PURE PLEASURE

Gary Thomas writes for all of us who sometimes feel guilty about
the good things God does for us. In *Pure Pleasure*, Gary helps us
understand that the abundant life Jesus promises in John 10:10 is a
better life than we could ever have imagined. And here is the good
news: It is not life after death, but life after birth!

> DR. DAVID JEREMIAH, senior pastor, Shadow Mountain
> Community Church, El Cajon, California

If Gary Thomas writes a book, you need to read it. It's as simple
as that. He has amazing insights into spiritual truths and is able
to make those truths graspable for all audiences. In *Pure Pleasure*,
Gary reminds us it is okay for Christians to feel good—even have
fun! A refreshing message at the right time for contemporary believers. You are going to enjoy this book.

> DR. ED YOUNG, senior pastor, Second Baptist Church,
> Houston, Texas

A theology of *pleasure*! What a great idea! And what a pleasure to
read. With all the verve and intelligence we've come to associate
with his entire body of work, Gary Thomas has taken to heart
Jeremy Taylor's warning that "God threatens terrible things if we
will not be happy." We all need this book—both the pleasure challenged and the pleasure prone, those who get it wrong and those
who don't get it at all. Joy is, after all, as C. S. Lewis put it, the
serious business of heaven.

> BEN PATTERSON, campus pastor, Westmont College,
> Santa Barbara, California

Gary's book is unlike anything I have ever read. He has stumbled on a hidden treasure of truth that will no doubt set many Christians free to experience God's richest blessings. Like *Sacred Marriage*, *Pure Pleasure* is a groundbreaking book that I would recommend to any Christian who desires to know more fully the heart of God.

Dr. Juli Slattery, family psychologist,
Focus on the Family, Colorado Springs, Colorado

As Gary Thomas so aptly demonstrates, *pure pleasure* is not a biblical oxymoron but rather a key characteristic of the God-honoring, soul-satisfying life. Warning of the dangers of both fleshly indulgence and an equally fleshly asceticism, Thomas guides our pursuit of holy delight by showing us how to embrace it in its fullness and maintain its connection to the pleasures in which God himself delights.

Randal Roberts, president and professor of spiritual
formation, Western Seminary, Portland, Oregon

Pure Pleasure will help you embrace and experience God, fullness of joy in his presence, and eternal pleasures at his right hand. I highly recommend it as essential reading for building a life of true pleasure and joy from a biblical perspective.

Siang-Yang Tan, PhD, professor of psychology,
Fuller Theological Seminary, Pasadena, California

This attention-keeping book will challenge, liberate, and inspire readers to worship God for every way he intended his children to celebrate his gifts of marriage, sex, family, money, time, laughter, joy, and exercise. Gary does a fantastic job of biblically balancing warnings against unhealthy pleasures with practical solutions for retaining the healthy ones.

Miles McPherson, senior pastor, Rock Church,
San Diego, California

PURE
PLEASURE

Books by Gary Thomas

Authentic Faith

Devotions for a Sacred Marriage

Devotions for Sacred Parenting

The Glorious Pursuit

Holy Available
(Previously titled *The Beautiful Fight*)

Pure Pleasure

Sacred Influence

Sacred Marriage

Sacred Parenting

Sacred Pathways

Seeking the Face of God

GARY THOMAS

Bestselling Author of *SACRED MARRIAGE*

PURE PLEASURE

WHY DO CHRISTIANS FEEL SO BAD
ABOUT FEELING GOOD?

ZONDERVAN®

ZONDERVAN.com/
AUTHORTRACKER
follow your favorite authors

ZONDERVAN

Pure Pleasure
Copyright © 2009 by Gary Thomas

This title is also available as a Zondervan ebook. Visit www.zondervan.com/ebooks.

This title is also available in a Zondervan audio edition. Visit www.zondervan.fm.

Requests for information should be addressed to:

Zondervan, *Grand Rapids, Michigan* 49530

Library of Congress Cataloging-in-Publication Data

Thomas, Gary (Gary Lee)
    Pure pleasure : why do Christians feel so bad about feeling good? / Gary Thomas.
      p. cm.
    Includes bibliographical references.
    ISBN 978-0-310-29080-3 (softcover)
    1. Pleasure—Religious aspects—Christianity. I. Title.
  BV4597.59T46 2009
  231.7—dc22
                                             2009009944

Published in association with Yates & Yates, www.yates2.com.

Interior design by Beth Shagene

Printed in the United States of America

09 10 11 12 13 14 15 • 24 23 22 21 20 19 18 17 16 15 14 13 12 11 10 9 8 7 6 5 4 3 2 1

To my parents, E.J. and Geneva Thomas

I was blessed to be raised by a mother
unusually sensitive to the Spirit's leading
and by a father who, well, put it this way:
If I ever attain half the character he has, my children will,
in the words of Scripture, "arise and call me blessed."
I have received more honors and accolades
in this world than I deserve,
but none as rich as being known as your son.

CONTENTS

1. The Tyranny of Torrential Thirst   11

2. Fortifying Ourselves with Pleasure   21

3. How Our Pleasure Pleases God   33

4. Enjoying the Earth without Loving the World   49

5. Party Like It's Biblical Time   71

6. Practical Pleasure   85

7. What's Your Pleasure?   103

8. Spiritual Ferns   119

9. Preserving Pleasure   133

10. Dangerous Pleasures   147

11. The Cost of Pleasure   167

12. Family Pleasure: Becoming a Servant of Their Joy   179

13. Singing in Exile: Finding Pleasure
    in Difficult Circumstances   195

14. Hilariously Holy   213

Epilogue   229

Acknowledgments   233

Notes   235

Online Video Small Group Discussion Questions   241

Chapter 1

THE TYRANNY OF TORRENTIAL THIRST

The way to be truly happy is to be truly human, and the way to be truly human is to be truly godly.

J. I. Packer

I commend the enjoyment of life.

Ecclesiastes 8:15

"Got ... to get ... some water!"

Houston sweltered in clammy humidity while the summer sun baked the streets with 95-degree heat. It was smack-dab in the middle of the afternoon, and every sane person sat cool and refreshed inside an air-conditioned house. Some no doubt felt startled by an eminently foolish, middle-aged, fluorescent-white man from the Pacific Northwest, melting in his running shoes as he trekked through the suburbs.

I had been invited by two churches to visit Texas. Since I was to preach on Sunday morning and then lead a staff retreat that evening, any run had to be shoehorned in on Sunday afternoon between the two morning sermons and the evening session.

Because of the heat, I planned to run just six miles. I took no water with me, but hey, the entire run would take less than fifty minutes; I figured, how thirsty could I get?

In less than fifteen minutes, I found out. Imagine chewing on hot sand for ten minutes, spitting it out, and then letting someone blow the air of a hair dryer directly down your throat for another five.

That's what it felt like.

Unfortunately, I still had another half hour to go.

Thirty minutes into my run, I felt like a ninety-year-old man. When a discarded, half-consumed bottle of Diet Coke lying in a ditch started to look inviting, I knew I was in trouble.

Finally, I saw a woman walking in front of her house, a house that—glory, hallelujah!—had a hose rolled up in front of it. I walked up to her and through a parched throat croaked out, "Excuse me; would you mind if I take a quick drink from your hose?"

"Not at all," she said, so I turned on the hose, let it run for a moment, and opened my mouth to receive—*the most plastic-tasting, mineral-encrusted water you can imagine.*

Think about it—the water in that hose had boiled inside a rubber tube for days. The bacteria were probably multiplying by the millisecond—no doubt falling over themselves in their rush to reproduce. As that water coursed down my throat, a small voice in the back of my mind said, "You're *so* going to pay for this. Three hours from now, you're going to wish you were dead."

But I didn't care. Fifty degrees *past* thirsty, I wanted immediate satisfaction. I would willingly risk any number of gastric nightmares just to wet my throat. So I kept drinking.

I finally made it back to my car, immediately drove to a local drugstore, and proceeded to buy an armload of icy beverages.

And then I smiled as I realized I had the perfect opening for my next book.

When Thirsty Trumps Trustworthy

When I drank from that hose, I *knew* I was flirting with disaster—but I didn't care. My intense thirst made me willing to risk long-term suffering for short-term satisfaction. Every scientist in the country could have lined up back to back and used charts, Power-Point presentations, anecdotes, personal testimonies, and research-tested data to demonstrate the foolishness of drinking that water, but I still might have put that hose to my lips and sucked down the liquid relief. I felt *that* thirsty. My urgent need trumped any other immediate concern.

My physical condition mirrored what many people face—spiritually, relationally, and emotionally. And spiritually thirsty people will put a lot of poison in their mouths, just to stop the thirst.

Nonbelievers are supernaturally thirsty because they do not know God, whom they were created to enjoy. Many believers are thirsty because they do not know how to enjoy God and the life he has given them. Some in the church feel suspicious, at best, of pleasure. We consider *pleasure* a synonym for *sin*. If it feels good, we think, it must be the devil's handmaiden. So we set up our lives on duty, responsibility, and obligation—good things all—with little true pleasure to season our days. Over time, these lives that are devoid of holy and good pleasure become extremely "thirsty," and we begin gravitating toward a release that is not holy or good or honoring to God—pleasures that war against our souls instead of building us up.

On Sunday morning as we sit in church listening to the pastor, the tyranny of our thirsty souls screams so loudly that we become all but deaf to wisdom, to warnings, even to Scripture about the ways in which we terrorize our souls with polluted pleasures. We may hear testimony after testimony about how our pet escape actually works as a trap, an insidious threshold to addiction, misery, and ruin; but if we're *really* thirsty, we may not care. When we allow ourselves to get *this* thirsty, we make ourselves vulnerable to any number of spiritual ills. We'll drink the poisoned water anyway.

I woke up this morning and had a big glass of water and a venti chai tea latte. From this vantage point, I could look back at myself those few months ago and say, "Gary, put the hose *down*." But that's because I wasn't thirsty this morning. From where I now sat, that half-empty bottle of diet Coke in the ditch looked absolutely gross. I wouldn't consider giving it a second glance. In fact, right now, the very hose seems repulsive. I could fault myself for taking a drink, but *wouldn't it be wiser to fault myself for allowing a situation to occur in which I became so thirsty that I reached the point of desperation?*

So let me ask you — from a spiritual, relational, emotional, and physical perspective — how thirsty do you feel as you read these words? Has your faith become all about obligation, duty, and responsibility? Do you find yourself occasionally shocked by something that looks inviting to you, something that you know should instead feel abhorrent? Does your lack of joy leave you achingly vulnerable to temptation?

Instead of persistently criticizing yourself for constantly giving in to such temptations, why not take a step back and figure out how to cultivate a life that will free you from the tyranny of your often-demanding thirst? Can you accept that there might be a holy purpose behind the intentional cultivation of appropriate pleasures?

Filled to the Brim

Rather than showcase a life of satisfaction, for years the church has tried to scare us out of our sin. For example, you could fortify yourself against an affair by meditating on all the evil that could result: the consequences of bringing home an STD; the shame of getting caught and exposed, perhaps risking your job or at least your reputation; the pain of seeing your spouse's hurt reaction; the horror of watching your kids lose their respect for you; or the threat of a revenge-minded spouse.

I suppose there's a place for this approach. If you lived *not* to sin, you might even be able to make a case that such an exercise would bring spiritual benefit.

Or...

You could focus on building a marriage in which thoughts of straying get pushed out by a real and satisfying intimacy in which no room exists for another lover. You could spend your time actively raising your children, becoming engaged in their lives in such a way that your heart overflows with love for your family, making any thought of tearing apart your family repugnant. You could faithfully pursue the work to which God has called you so that you have neither the time nor the inclination for something as sordid as an affair.

See the difference? We can build lives of true, lasting pleasure and so fortify ourselves against evil because evil has lost much of its allure—or we can try, with an iron will, to "scare" ourselves away from evil while still, deep in our hearts, truly longing for it.

Which life do you want to live?

Which life do you believe will ultimately succeed?

Thomas Chalmers, a nineteenth-century Scottish preacher, called the former method (meditating on the "vanity" of sin) "altogether incompetent and ineffectual." He believed that the "constitution of our nature" demands that we instead focus on the "rescue and recovery" of our heart from wrong affections by embracing the "expulsive power of a new affection."[1]

In a similar way, G. K. Chesterton* wrote that "the great gap in modern ethics" is "the absence of vivid pictures of purity and spiritual triumph."[2] In other words, we need to preach the glory of a truly soul-satisfying life instead of sounding obsessed about the

---

*G. K. Chesterton (1874–1936)) was a British poet, journalist, novelist, and spiritual writer best known for his Father Brown mysteries, his biography of Francis of Assisi, and his spiritual classic, *Orthodoxy*. His work greatly influenced the conversion, and later the writings, of C. S. Lewis.

dangers of a life lived foolishly. We can send our kids off to college with horrid tales of drunken students falling to their deaths from third-floor balconies, show them charts that demonstrate the percentage of sexually active college students who carry at least one sexually transmitted disease, share testimonies of the soul-destroying effects of the love of money—or we can build into them a vision of the unique soul-satisfaction that comes from being an instrument used by God, of the opportunities to build relationships with people who may become lifelong friends, and of the glory of becoming equipped to enter the life profession God created them to fulfill.

I want my children to fill their lives with *good* things, which in turn will help them to disdain the bad. I want to capture their hearts with "vivid pictures of purity and spiritual triumph" instead of trying to scare them away from soul-destroying habits.

"Where freedom is near," a theologian once wrote, "the chains begin to hurt."[3] Jesus' more pleasurable way of *life* showcases the agony of the way of *death*. When we unashamedly preach true, holy, and God-honoring pleasure, then the sordidness of sin, the foolishness of spiritual rebellion, and the agony of addictions become shockingly apparent.

Chalmers would argue that an "old affection"—a sinful desire—is "almost never" overcome by the sheer force of "mental determination." That is, sin almost always eventually gets a young man or woman who is merely "determined" not to fall. The nineteenth-century preacher would say that mental reasoning ("I know I shouldn't"; "This could end badly"; "My parents would get so angry"; "This might affect my future") cannot possibly compete with the force of our passions. "But what cannot be thus *destroyed* may be *dispossessed*—and one taste may be made to give way to another, and to lose its power entirely as the reigning affection of the mind. It is thus that the boy ceases to be the slave of his appetite."[4]

Let's return to my original story. I *knew* that drinking from the hot Houston hose amounted to a dicey proposition, but I didn't care. I needed *something* to conquer my thirst. College students, single moms, middle-aged men, and elderly widows need something too. Let's give them visions of something *better*, something nobler, to fill their hearts. Let's set the church on the path of exalting "vivid pictures of purity and spiritual triumph." Let's advertise the good life by becoming living examples of truly satisfied souls.

Spiritual triumph begins and ends with finding our satisfaction in God above all things. We serve a generous God, however, who eagerly wants to bless us with many other pleasures, gifts from his hand, that delight us—and in delighting us, bring pleasure back to him. Rather than seeing these gifts as competitors that steal our hearts from God, perhaps we can gratefully receive them and allow God to use them to ruin us to the ways of the world.

Prayer and fellowship are among life's richest pleasures, but let's not stop there. Let us learn to fill our souls with beauty, art, noble achievement, fine meals, rich relationships, and soul-cleansing laughter. When we acknowledge these pleasures, we acknowledge God as a genius creator of brilliant inventions. Let us be wary of a faith that denies these blessings as "worldly" and unfit, as though Satan rather than God had designed them. Let us refuse to fall into the enemy's trap of denying ourselves God's good pleasures so that we end up deeply vulnerable to illicit pleasure.

In truth, God created us first for *his* own pleasure, not our own; but when we live a life of holy pleasure, we do bring pleasure to God (see chapter 3). In this context and with this understanding, pleasure can become a powerful force for piety and goodness.

The Place for Pleasure

This book asks how we might recapture pleasure in the Christian life. Wouldn't you like to explore the potential of building a life of healthy pleasure? If God designed healthy pleasure to sustain us, how can you become better equipped to receive the strength of such pleasures? Would you like to better understand how God delights to see his children live in pleasure, just as any father loves to sit back and watch his children squeal with delight on Christmas morning?

If your life has been all about obligation, responsibility, and denial, you're in for an eye-opening treat. If you've become dangerously thirsty, vulnerable to any number of soul-numbing temptations, you're about to be fortified against sin. If your life has lost its appeal and your heart has lost its joy, get ready for a new awakening.

Perhaps you have never connected your pleasure with God and have set up a wall between what we might call "creational" pleasures and worship. We'll do our best to tear down that wall. Or maybe you're facing an entirely different battle. You've become a slave to your pleasures. You never or rarely say no to pleasure, and you need help to put pleasure in its proper place and perspective. There's something here for you as well.

Are you ready to explore what may seem threatening to some — namely, what if pleasure can lead us *to* God instead of compete *with* God?

≡ DISCUSSION AND REFLECTION ≡

1. Gary talks about becoming so thirsty on a run that he was willing to drink water that might make him sick. Instead of simply faulting himself for taking the drink, however, he thinks he should be faulted for putting himself in a situation where he became so desperate he didn't care about the consequences. How is this analogy helpful when it comes to handling temptation and addiction?

2. Prior to reading this book, when you heard or thought about pleasure, did your mind immediately roam to illicit enjoyments? Why do you think the word *pleasure* is so often used to describe sinful desires?

3. Do you agree with Gary that it's more helpful to fill our lives with good and godly desires, and thereby reduce (though not eliminate) our desire for illicit pleasure, or do you think this approach is certain to fail? What would be an alternative approach?

4. Has pleasure had too large, or too small, a role in your life? What do you think has contributed to this?

Chapter 2

FORTIFYING OURSELVES WITH PLEASURE

We cannot grow spiritually if we ignore our humanness, just as we cannot become fully human if we ignore spirituality.

Jean Vanier

To the pure, all things are pure, but to those who are corrupted and do not believe, nothing is pure. In fact, both their minds and consciences are corrupted.

Titus 1:15

If you were a Christian in the 1980s, you probably remember the "Ungame." It became all the rage for about six weeks, until we discovered how truly boring it was. The name says it all. It implies that just having fun isn't a worthy pastime; we have to make it meaningful, "spiritual," and purposeful.

So we'll call it the "*Un*game."

Leave it to Christians to spoil even Monopoly.

Earlier generations had it even worse. In her classic work *To Kill a Mockingbird*, author Harper Lee recounts how "foot-washing Baptists" condemned Miss Maudie to hell for spending too much time with her flowers. Miss Maudie explained to Scout:

> "Foot-washers believe anything that's pleasure is a sin. Did you know some of 'em came out of the woods one Saturday and passed by this place and told me me and my flowers were going to hell?"

"Your flowers too?"

"Yes, ma'am. They'd burn right with me. They thought I spent too much time in God's outdoors and not enough time inside the house reading the Bible."[1]

Cultural prejudice, not biblical teaching, creates this undercurrent against pleasure for pleasure's sake. When Jesus said he came to give us an abundant life (John 10:10), he spoke not so much about *length* of life as about *quality* of life. One writer puts it this way: "It is not true that Jesus was interested only in life after death. His message was aimed at life after birth."[2] Eugene Peterson in *The Message* translates John 10:10, "I came so they can have real and eternal life, more and better life than they ever dreamed of."

In the next couple of chapters, I'll lay out a fuller biblical defense of embracing pleasure as a pathway to worship and intimacy with God. For now, I want to make a crucial point. Here's where I think the church has gotten off track: We often fail to make the distinction that Paul makes when he wrote to Titus, "To the pure, all things are pure, but to those who are corrupted and do not believe, nothing is pure. In fact, both their minds and consciences are corrupted" (1:15).

In other words, *redemption*—becoming a believer, being born again, whatever language you prefer—*means something.* In context, Paul is arguing against hyper-religionists trying to saddle Christians with arbitrary rules and prohibitions. These teachers wanted to enslave believers to the old belief that if a defiled person touches something (food, drink, or even another person), this something also becomes defiled. Paul cleverly turns this around, saying if someone is pure, then whatever they touch becomes pure!

I'm arguing that we need to look at pleasure and the good gifts of this earth through the eyes of redemption. When our hearts are cleansed and transformed by God, the very things that used to cause us to stumble can now become friends of faith. Not *all* things, of course; anything specifically against the will and commands of God, regardless of what kind of pleasure it seems to offer, will always destroy our souls. But the good things of this earth, created by God to be received with thanksgiving and praise—things such as friendship, good food and fine drinks, laughter, sex, and family life—can be redeemed to season our life and faith in many positive ways. God can even give us the power to take what we formerly misused and transform it into an instrument of praise.

The challenge we face, of course, is that redemption remains incomplete this side of heaven. The sin nature still works within us (Romans 7:14–25). I'm *not* suggesting that we can "pleasure" our way out of temptation, because with a sin-weakened heart, if I'm presented with two pleasures—one healthy and one destructive—I am likely to choose the wrong one.

Embracing pleasure must always begin with a heart being renewed by God's Holy Spirit.

Once this powerful act of redemption has begun, by God's grace and mercy those in Christ can embrace and even cultivate pleasure in such a way that we become less vulnerable to the allure of sin and temptation. Embracing pleasure instead of remaining suspicious of it is no cure-all, but it can become an effective tool, provided our hearts have been (and are being) changed.

Neither am I suggesting that pleasure is a sufficient tool in and of itself. Because we all have sin-stained hearts, the ancient lessons about our need for the spiritual disciplines, sacrifice, self-denial, mortification, and detachment still apply. Without these, I am a fool to generously embrace pleasure, because in only a matter of time that pleasure will consume me. With these spiritual practices, however—and while enjoying the benefits of a redeemed life, the active counsel of God's Holy Spirit, and the support of God's community (the local church)—I can begin to truly enjoy life, perhaps for the very first time. I can embrace pleasure as a way to celebrate God and the life he has given me. Pleasure can lead me *to* him instead of *away* from him.

In a progressive journey of faith, God gradually re-centers our desires toward *holy* pleasures, spiritually good and healthy things that leave us satisfied and full, so that sin begins to lose much (but never all) of its appeal. So often we assume that "pleasure" means something illicit—so we warn others against the dangers of pleasure. But if we learn to redeem pleasure and allow our hearts to be shaped by the Creator of all that is good, pleasure can become the servant of holiness, not its enemy.

Self-Hating Christians

It becomes a spiritual sickness when we denounce pleasure simply because it feels pleasurable. In point of fact, doing so is a form of self-hatred and an offense to the gospel of love. Author Karen Horney warns of our "taboos on enjoyment," and when she does so, I wonder how many Christians you know (perhaps yourself!) *who are just like this*:

> He wants to go on a trip, and the inner voice says: "You don't deserve it." Or, in other situations: "You have no right to rest, or to go to a movie, or to buy a dress." Or, in an even more general sense: "Good things are not for you." ... After having done a good day's work, he is tired and wants to rest. The voice says: "You are just lazy." "No, I am really tired." "Oh, no, that is sheer self-indulgence; this way you will never get anywhere." And after such a back and forth he either takes a rest with a guilty conscience or forces himself to continue working—without deriving any benefit either way.[3]

I have lived through this! What a cleverly demonic attack; what an effective way to wear out every one of God's workers and limit our witness while destroying our joy.

Here's the reality: Satan will trap some with compulsions toward illicit pleasures. These traps are well known and preached against every week. But other believers tend toward prideful, work-oriented compulsions in which *any* rest or *any* enjoyment is seen as weakness or "giving in." Since God didn't make us to live in sin *or* without pleasure, either way of life will eventually destroy us.

The way Satan piles guilt upon guilt can be devastatingly effective and amazingly clever. Sometimes he'll even use religious compulsion or appeal to our social conscience: "If people in another country are starving, how dare I spend three dollars on a cup of coffee?" A social conscience is a good and holy thing—and if we spend more on coffee than we do in reaching out to the hurting, our priorities may well be skewed. In that case, it could be the Holy Spirit convicting us rather than the devil tempting us. The basic principle, however, is this: our self-imposed misery doesn't erase someone else's misery; on the contrary, it may simply increase God's displeasure. What pleasure do we think God—our loving Father—derives from us hating and/or abusing ourselves? How do we honor him when we deny ourselves everything he created to bring us pleasure?*

Fortified by Satisfaction

Just recently I had a very good day. It began with a rich time of Bible reading, prayer, and study, followed by a productive session of

---

*This isn't to deny the real problem of consumerism and selfish, wanton consumption. We'll wrestle with this in chapter 11. However, it is simplistic to suggest that the problems of poverty are rooted in the failure of Christians to give more. In many cases, the problem is systemic and governmental, and until these roots are addressed, more money alone won't feed the hungry.

writing. Then my wife greeted me with a glorious time of physical intimacy (the first time we had been alone in the house for quite some time; when you have three teenagers, you take what you can get!). I followed that up with a meeting with a local pastor at Starbucks. We talked about life, about running, about theology, about church. I returned home and set out on a beautiful early-autumn run, leaving in time so that I'd return by the time the kids got home from school.

By late afternoon, my heart was overflowing with joy. Mental stimulation, vocational fulfillment, sexual intimacy, rich Christian fellowship, a well-made chai tea, physical exercise—I felt like the most blessed person on the face of the earth. With my heart so full, what could sin offer me? Any evil would be a step back. My intimacy with God in the morning gave me infinitely more fulfillment than watching an inane television program. Sex with my wife helped maintain our relationship, strengthened my family's bond, and helped secure stability for my children—why would I allow illicit sex to undo all that? The conversation with the pastor inspired both of us; it honored God and served each other. Why would I ever want to gossip when I can encourage and be encouraged? And since I believe (as I'll develop in my next book) that a direct connection exists between physical fitness and spiritual fitness, the training run helped feed my spirit and fight off any number of spiritual ills. Because I've experienced the benefits of keeping in shape firsthand, a life of sloth holds little appeal.

Now, not every day reaches such glorious and pleasurable heights. Some days begin with evil and seem to end with evil. At the conclusion of those days, however, I want to recapture another day that begins and ends with faith, not remember the evil day. By the grace of God, this very thing can happen as he forgives, redeems, and empowers. I don't want to overstate the power of pleasure. Because of the residual sin nature within me, I will never face a life of no temptation; and because of my weakness, I will never, this side of heaven, reach moral perfection. I won't even smell it.

But I can begin to develop a taste for it. True God-honoring pleasure can help me do that.

Theologian D. A. Carson warns, "The sad fact is that many people dwell on dirt without grasping that it is dirt. The wise Christian will see plenty of dirt in the world, but will recognize it as dirt, precisely because everything that is clean has captured his or her mind."[4]

When we cultivate the "clean," we begin to see dirt for what it is: dirt! Medical studies have shown that losing our temper and living with an angry undercurrent assault our cardiovascular system and also create distance in our relationships. Materialism will cause us to miss what matters most in life. Materialists may enter retirement financially secure, but they will likely also feel estranged from their families and lack true friends with whom they can spend their money. Gluttony will ultimately create physical pain and slow us down. Pride will rob us of intimacy by making it difficult for others to get close to us and by keeping us from becoming honest and authentic.

In this life, Christ-followers remain susceptible to sin and temptation, but note the difference. We will hate sin even as it tempts us (see Romans 7:14 – 25). We see the "dark roots" underneath temptation's dye job and realize how fake the allure really is.

Name a sin and you identify a serious threat to true, abundant life. Name a spiritual failing and you recognize a vicious attack on a fulfilling life. I love Julian of Norwich's take on this.* She says that the God-touched soul begins to hate the vileness of sin more

---

* Julian of Norwich was a famous fourteenth-century anchorite who wrote the classic *Revelations of Divine Love*. An anchorite was a medieval layperson who sought extreme isolation, "anchored" to one area or church, so that she could pursue God through a life of penance, prayer, and purity of heart.

than it hates hell. Instead of being dissuaded merely by the eternal consequences of sin, we open our eyes to the inherent maliciousness of sin—and so we lose our taste for it. She warns that those who focus primarily on the *punishment* of sin get distracted from focusing on friendship with God.[5] In practical, modern terms, she pleads with us, "Let God win you over with his joy, pleasure, and friendship, and you'll be that much less vulnerable to being fooled by the *counterfeit* pleasure of sin." In terms of spiritual warfare, she points out that our enemy, "the Fiend," loses more by our rising than he ever gains by our falling.

Jesus came promising the good life.

And yet why do Christians focus primarily on rejecting the bad life?

A Pure Party

A marvelous passage in 1 Kings describes Solomon's dedication of God's temple. He offered thousands of fellowship offerings to the Lord, eaten by the people. Imagine a generous potluck to which you had to bring nothing. The king supplied it all. Now notice this:

> They celebrated it [the Feast of Tabernacles] before the LORD our God for seven days and seven days more, fourteen days in all. On the following day he [Solomon] sent the people away. They blessed the king and then went home, joyful and glad in heart for all the good things the LORD had done for his servant David and his people Israel.
>
> 1 Kings 8:65–66

Did you catch that? They feasted, celebrated, and rejoiced for fourteen days. When they finally went home, they had joyful and glad hearts. *Fourteen days of celebration!* In many Christian churches, people feel guilty for celebrating for fourteen *minutes*. If you throw one feast, at least one somber saint will complain,

"Shouldn't we fast and give all this to the poor?" If a church decides to spend a little money to do a fun activity, someone will piously confront the pastor, inquiring, "Wouldn't it be better to stay home and pray for our missionaries and send that money to them?"

We have largely lost the concept of creating inviting communities in which people get built up with joy, strengthened in celebration, and nurtured in holy pleasure. We must not, we cannot, neglect the poor or lose our zeal for mission outreach. But in the same way, for the sake of honoring God, securing our children's faith, and supporting our own witness, we must not, and cannot, neglect celebrating God's goodness and faithfulness.

The rate at which we are losing our young people should alarm every church in this country. Some estimates put the loss at 75 percent. Many experts are trying to find out why kids raised in church abandon it in their twenties. Here's a clue: If teens think they have to leave the church to celebrate, why would they ever want to stay? If every time they enter the walls dedicated to God's service they hear *only* about their shortcomings, their obligations, and their irresponsibility, what would make them want to come back?

I'm *not* saying we shouldn't confront the sin of the young. Of course we should. Their sins—including their selfishness and apathy—need to be challenged. *But let's preach the good life every bit as much as we warn them away from the path of destruction.* Let's invite them to drink from the well that truly satisfies, and then let's live it so that they see with their own eyes the glory and happiness of an obedient Christian.

As a parent and as a Christian, I believe that God calls me to live a life of satisfaction in him so that my kids see how grateful I am, how pleased I am, how satisfied I am, in Christ. I walk with God because he is the true Creator and rightful Lord. But I also walk with Christ because a life with Christ is a beautiful life, the most incredible journey I can imagine. My kids know of the money we give to God's work. They witness the stress that ministry brings into our home. They notice the sacrifices of serving Christ. But more than that—above all that—they see the hearts of their mom and dad filled with joy because we can imagine no better life than the one lived in fellowship with God and in obedience to his Word and his will.

Because some "headliner" Christians allow themselves to get wooed away from true pleasure and so get caught by corrupted passions, the world tends to think of Christians as pathetic creatures who deny their true desires, live hypocritical lives, and indulge in secret what they denounce in public. Undercutting the importance of pure and holy pleasure hinders our witness. We try to invite people into the faith with our words; let's also begin inviting them into the faith with our lives and with our sincerely satisfied souls.

But an even better reason exists to embrace pure pleasure, one that goes beyond helping us live satisfied lives and find strength to resist temptation: *our pleasure brings pleasure to God.* Let's explore this next.

DISCUSSION AND REFLECTION

1. How does becoming a Christian change what we take pleasure in?

2. What "taboos on enjoyment" did you grow up with? How does someone begin to reevaluate arbitrary rules that aren't based in Scripture?

3. Why do you think Christians often focus on Scriptures that talk about self-denial and prohibitions but remain silent about passages, such as 1 Kings 8, that talk about divine celebrations?

4. How can celebrating and enjoying this world make us stronger as believers?

Chapter 3

How Our Pleasure Pleases God

The LORD be exalted, who delights in the well-being of his servant.

Psalm 35:27

God wishes us to take true pleasure with him in our salvation, and in this he wishes us to be greatly comforted and strengthened, and so he wants our souls to be happily filled with this, through his grace; for we are his delight; he takes pleasure in us eternally, and so shall we in him, through his grace.

Julian of Norwich

Karen Kingsbury.

Angela Hunt.

Oh! A Melody Carlson! Gotta get that one!

I know the names of all these authors, though I have read none of their books. Even so, I once returned from a publishing convention with almost two dozen Christian novels, eagerly anticipating the look on my oldest daughter's face when I handed them over. I didn't plan to read a single one myself, but parents will agree with me when I say that few things give a mom or dad more pleasure than seeing their kid truly enjoy something. My daughter Allison used to devour those novels like I salivate over a brand-new pair of running shoes.

I couldn't wait to get the books into her hands.

Watch a young mom play with her baby. Most mothers become

enthralled when they first get their babies to laugh. They can't help themselves; they'll spend a half hour trying to elicit one last giggle, because the sound of a child learning to giggle feels absolutely intoxicating. It's life with a capital *L*.

All of this merely reflects the heavenly Parent above us all. As our true and perfect Father, God delights in our delight. Isaiah 62:4–5 reads, "The LORD will take delight [i.e., *pleasure*] in you ...; as a bridegroom rejoices over his bride, so will your God rejoice over you."

The psalms proclaim a generous God who loves to give his creatures things that bring delight:

> He makes grass grow for the cattle,
>   and plants for man to cultivate—
>   bringing forth food from the earth:
> wine that gladdens the heart of man,
>   oil to make his face shine,
>   and bread that sustains his heart....
>
> When you give it to them,
>   they gather it up;
> when you open your hand,
>   they are satisfied with good things.
>
> Psalm 104:14–15, 28

Those close to God's heart embraced this truth with unparalleled exuberance. In spite of the many troubles he passed through, King David never lost the sense that God always sought his best: "The LORD be exalted, *who delights in the well-being of his servant*" (Psalm 35:27, emphasis added). In a very moving passage, David testifies, "He [God] brought me out into a spacious place; he rescued me *because he delighted in me*" (2 Samuel 22:20, emphasis added).

When God calls Israel to obedience, he does so with the promise of pleasure: "'Return to me, and I will return to you,' says the LORD

Almighty.... 'Then all the nations will call you blessed, for yours will be a delightful land,' says the Lord Almighty" (Malachi 3:7, 12).

The Bible is clear: "The Lord takes pleasure in those who fear him, in those who hope in his steadfast love" (Psalm 147:11 ESV). Enjoying God and what he has created (in the way he intends us to enjoy it) brings pleasure to God. It is the pathway to worship and increases our spiritual vigor: "[The Lord] satisfies your desires with good things so that your youth is renewed like the eagle's" (Psalm 103:5).

Even famous ascetics, such as Julian of Norwich — who once eagerly prayed for God to bring more pain into her life — understood how much delight God takes in our pleasure. After believing that Jesus told her, "I ask nothing more of you for my hardship but that I give you pleasure," Julian goes on to say:

> A glad giver pays little attention to the thing he is giving, but his whole desire and intention is to please and comfort the one to whom he gives it; and if the receiver values the gift highly and takes it gratefully, then the generous giver thinks nothing of all his hardship and the price he had to pay, because of the joy and delight that he feels at having pleased and comforted the one he loves.[1]

If all of this is true — and I believe it is — then a gospel that speaks only of duty and discipline robs God of pleasure. Jesus paid the highest price on the cross to (in part) enable us to laugh, to set us free to enjoy the world instead of becoming enslaved by it. So we do him no favors by acting as though his work on the cross somehow came up short as a sacrifice.* *He died to give us life. When*

---

*This isn't to deny that, *primarily*, Jesus died to absorb the wrath that would otherwise be poured out on us (the emphasis of Reformed theology) and to defeat Satan and the powers of death (the emphasis of Eastern Orthodox teaching). I am, admittedly, talking about one of the "fringe benefits" of the cross, not its central purpose.

we reject that life, we reject the benefits of his sacrifice of death. This doesn't honor him; it grieves him. Religion tempts us to become more concerned with our pride-laced denial and self-exalting piety than with bringing delight to our heavenly Father, who takes pleasure in our pleasure—pleasure won at an inconceivably high cost. As David testified, and we echo, "He rescued me *because he delighted in me.*"

The God of Pleasure

Once, while walking through a McDonald's restaurant, I saw eight ten-year-old girls celebrating a birthday. Each of their faces wore a smile. The warmth of sheer, unadulterated happiness permeated the gathering.

It was as if a light had been turned on and I could see God's pleasure, his delight, in this scene. God felt happy that these girls were happy. Their delight, their joy, even their giddiness, gave God great pleasure.

Have you ever thought about that—that you can give God great pleasure by enjoying yourself?

If you're a parent, you shouldn't find this difficult to do. Imagine being on vacation, watching your children laugh and play. Imagine Christmas morning as the young kids tear into the presents. Does anything make you happier? Don't moments like these break into the dull routines of life and give us a glimpse of heaven?

That's the image of God in you—taking joy in the joy of your children.

The fact that we are children of God—and that Jesus urges us to become like children—speaks of a certain demeanor, a certain delight, a certain trust in God's goodness and favor toward us. Children love to play. The thought of children forced to work in a factory or to toil all day long in the hot sun appalls us—we've passed laws to prevent it. And while God's servants are not merely his children (he also calls us to sacrificial and mature service), we never become *less* than his children. And healthy children often engage in play.

Now, contrast children with certain teenagers and adults who sometimes hold back from play for fear of being embarrassed or looking unstylish or "uncool." They sacrifice their own pleasure on the altar of pride.

An uninhibited and holy joy erupts in the *humility* of childlike play.

How does your faith response — your attitude, your demeanor — honor or dishonor God? Has your approach to life been an act of worship that makes God laugh and clap his hands with glee while he watches you, or one that makes him shake his head and whisper, "I really wish so-and-so would lighten up. What kind of example is he setting for my kingdom?"

When the church teaches a glum faith of responsibility, a faith devoid of joy; when the pulpit treats pleasure like some kind of spiritual leprosy; when people of faith speak as though they are antisex, antihumor, antifun, anti anything that brings pleasure, we risk fostering the kind of devotion that the Bible shockingly and without reservation rejects.

I want to enjoy intimacy with my wife, because when we treasure each other's bodies — bodies that God created and designed — we put a smile on God's face. I want to stop and enjoy a sunset and let it expand my soul, because in doing so I'm celebrating God's handiwork. I want to revel in a well-written novel, because devouring a work of excellence is to acknowledge God's inspiration and gift-giving wisdom. I want to thank God for a good meal instead of seeing it as a temptation, because I'd hate it — absolutely despise it — if I gave an expensive gift to my child and she immediately asked,

"Are you sure you can afford this?" or "I'm not worthy to receive it; take it back."

Do you see how living only out of duty robs our heavenly Father of great pleasure? I did not write this book solely to encourage Christians to embrace pleasure. That's a secondary aim. My first aim is to give God pleasure by helping his children to receive and celebrate *his* pleasure.

Connecting our pleasure with God—even seeing pleasure as a legitimate and blessed pathway to worship—builds our souls and strengthens our devotion. Pleasure divorced from God leads to pain and misery. Looking at our pleasure as a way to please God slowly begins to shape what we take pleasure in.

Whatever Gets You through the Night ...

"Sandra" feels ignored by her husband and secretly has occasional regrets about giving up a well-paying job to stay home with her three children, who never seem content. They always want *something more.* And her husband—don't even get her started talking about his sense of entitlement!

She told me of the evening she had spent with her sister, enjoying a glass of wine as they talked about their families. The conversation stoked the emotional pain, turning a low-burning irritation into a flaming ache. Sandra asked for a second glass of wine. She explained, "I'm not a big girl, and I hadn't had anything to eat"—which was her way of preparing me for the confession, "So actually I got a little drunk."

While soul-building, God-affirming pleasure pleases our Father and brings him pleasure, our tendency to use pleasure to dull the pain makes him grieve. He wants us to turn to *him.* The trap of pleasure divorced from God's governing hand will lead to our ruin: "He who loves pleasure will become poor" (Proverbs 21:17).

In 2 Timothy 3:4, Paul warns against "lovers of pleasure rather than lovers of God." This passage challenges those who pursue pleasure as their primary aim *rather than* the God-ordained path of pursuing God and finding pleasure as a by-product of a life lived in surrender to Christ's purposes and aims.

Pleasure divorced from God's governing hand becomes treacherous. Frank Sinatra became famous for saying, "I'm for anything that gets you through the night, be it prayer, tranquilizers, or a bottle of Jack Daniels," a sentiment echoed by John Lennon when he sang, "Whatever gets you thru the night, 'salright, 'salright ..."[2]

No, it's *not* all right. Some pleasures affirm, rebuild, refresh, and enhance life, honoring God the Creator and pleasing him at the same time. Others destroy life, causing us harm and him grief. We become most vulnerable when we are desperate—and that's precisely when we need to take the most care about our choice of pleasures. It's not merely about getting through the night; it's about what helps us *grow* through *life*, pointing us toward *eternity*.

If you misuse creature comforts to "get through the night," you'll soon find yourself using that same pleasure to "get through a challenging week," and eventually you'll rely on what has become a crutch to "weather a difficult year." In time, you'll wake up to discover that pleasure has become your pain, perhaps even a source of addiction.

Especially in the land of enjoyment, our motivation must come from what Paul describes in 2 Corinthians 5:9: "So we make it our goal to please him [the Lord]." If my pleasures don't give pleasure to God, then eventually I will have to choose either to change my pleasures or to change my god. A soul can't serve two masters. That's why I want Christians to connect pleasure *with* God rather than see the two as enemies. The best protection against the misuse of creature comforts and enjoyments is to see them as something we receive from God. If you divorce your pleasure from God, that pleasure, initially designed by God as a friend of faith, will turn into a cunning enemy.

The book of Proverbs presents pleasure in two lights — as a trap that can lead to our ruin (21:17; 14:13) *or* as a gift from God that demonstrates his blessing and favor (10:28). Depending on the translation you use, you might feel confused when you look up these passages. The NIV chooses to translate a single Hebrew word (*śimḥâ*) as "pleasure" when it addresses negative connotations (as in Proverbs 21:17) and as "joy" when it refers to positive connotations (10:28). In this light, you *could* translate Proverbs 10:28, "The prospect of the righteous is pleasure."

Compassionate Concern

Even when we choose our pleasures poorly, God grieves *as a father* — an important truth. Becoming a father myself has helped me to understand my heavenly Father's compassionate concern. Because of the cross — because our divine King defeated Satan and death while pouring out his wrath on Jesus instead of on us — every thought God has toward his redeemed children flows out of his tender mercy. Can you think of any more comforting words for the redeemed than these: "If God is for us, who can be against us?" (Romans 8:31)? The Lord is *for* us. "Therefore, there is now *no condemnation* for those who are in Christ Jesus (8:1, emphasis added).

So when we misuse pleasure to escape the pain of life and the ache of our disappointments, God still looks tenderly at us because he is our Father and we are his dearly loved adopted children. He looks at our spiritual panic and sees us as travelers lost in the woods who, instead of thinking clearly, in a frenzy push deeper into the woods and get themselves even more lost. He feels sad at our predicament and grieves that we continue to make things worse.

Yet even here, God doesn't condemn the pleasure; he grieves

its *misuse*. Yes, he will gently discipline us (Hebrews 12:5–11). At times he will ask us to deny ourselves what could be legitimate pleasures because he knows we can't handle them. You take away belts from those on suicide watch, not because there is anything wrong with a belt, but because the mentally distressed could use that helpful belt to hang themselves.

The divine prohibition *is always an act of love and concern*. It is never malicious teasing. It is never based on a desire to deny his children any good gift simply to taunt them. God does the denying only with passionate feelings of overwhelming care and compassion. The first time we re-embrace that pleasure, God smiles. When you see a man formerly on a suicide watch now wearing a belt, you feel joy that he has regained the mental health to be able to wear it.

Some of us dishonor God by the way we think he withholds, forbids, and plays with our pleasures. *He is our Father.* He loves us. He delights in watching us enjoy what he has made, which is why we can so openly embrace pleasure. Even when he asks us to deny something because we have misused it, he acts out of a parental commitment of love and concern.

The Gift That Keeps On Giving

At age four, our son decided he wanted to pick out a Mother's Day gift all by himself—no more scribbling his mark on a present picked out by his dad. No—he intended to get it himself.

Graham settled on the cheesiest piggy bank ever made. Normally my wife would roll her eyes and laugh at such a pink monstrosity; she has zero tolerance for tacky presents that clutter up the house. But when she opened this present, she cried genuine tears of joy. She knew this present came from Graham, and she felt so touched by the thought and gesture that the tackiness didn't faze her. She even put it on her nightstand in our bedroom. Graham wore a hundred-watt smile when he saw Lisa's tears. Nothing made him happier than to give a present that delighted his mom so much that it made her cry.

God, as the giver of many gifts, would love to see us cry tears of joy and gratitude when he gives us gifts that bring us pleasure. If you see this world and your life as a gift from a loving Creator, *and every Christian should*, then let's honor that gift by enjoying it. God has given us taste buds, nerve endings, the capacity to laugh, the ability to create, eyes to marvel, minds to wonder, noses to smell, and hands to feel. We give back to him in proportion to how much we enjoy these good gifts. When one of his gifts obviously moves us — as Graham's did my wife — then we bring a smile to God the giver's face.

The first recorded words God spoke to humans introduced a gift: "Be fruitful and increase in number; fill the earth and subdue it. Rule over ... every living creature.... I *give you* every seed-bearing plant on the face of the whole earth and every tree that has fruit with seed in it. They will be yours for food" (Genesis 1:28–29, emphasis added).

Do you think he might be waiting for us, perhaps for the first time in our lives, to truly open up the gift of life and savor it? While we busy ourselves trying to serve God, do you think he might wait for us to honor him by relishing the world he has made?

God-Colored Pleasures

Rooting pleasure in God not only shapes what we take pleasure in; eventually it even allows us to *enjoy* what might seem (to the unredeemed) like sacrifice. One of the United States' founding mothers, Abigail Adams, endured years of separation from her husband, John, while he represented overseas the colonies and then the young United States. Someone once asked Abigail if she would have allowed John to leave had she known beforehand how long he would stay away. She responded, "I feel a pleasure in being able to sacrifice my selfish passions to the general good."[3]

If our decision to embrace pleasure focuses on giving pleasure to God, then what gives us pleasure will ultimately reveal our spiritual maturity and the depth of our relationship with him. To the unformed soul, immediate feelings of pleasure represent the quickest and surest path to pleasure; to the child of God, pleasure becomes the destination we reach when we walk the path of obedience. Pleasure is the end result of a process more than it is a feeling, which is why we can take as much pleasure in sacrifice as we do in having fun.

Walking this journey for any significant period gradually shapes our hearts to look for the "deeper" side of pleasure rather than the surface, appearance-oriented pleasures that used to captivate us. Which of the following statements, for example, strike you as most honoring to God?

- "I have a nice car," *or* "I enjoy driving."
- "Look at my book collection," *or* "Let me tell you how a book has recently challenged me."
- "Guess which college my kid got into?" *or* "I love spending time with my kids."
- "I have an important job," *or* "I enjoy my work."
- "I have a really expensive house in a nice neighborhood," *or* "I delight in relaxing at home in my favorite chair [or out in my garden]."
- "Look how attractive, important, capable [fill in the blank] my spouse is," *or* "I know my wife intimately and enjoy her company."

A vital relationship with God colors our pleasures with a holy passion and leads us to value relationship over the spirit of possession, intimacy over ambition, and service over selfishness. God sets us free to revel in what he has designed for our enjoyment; and eventually, as we mature, we begin to detest what goes against his nature and will.

We do not need to fear pleasure; we need to fear the *alienation from God* that corrupts our sense of pleasure and that makes the pleasure drive so potentially dangerous.

It comes down to this: I embrace pleasure because the Bible commands me to. But my immediate pleasure, my sense of happiness, never becomes my greatest aim. More than anything, I want to glorify God. When I embrace creational delights as a way to honor God, I become a better steward of pleasure while also remembering that pleasure isn't my highest aim. As a dad, I revel in watching my kids laugh and enjoy themselves, but I feel even prouder when I see our children act selflessly and with great courage.

This feeling of pride came on my wife and me recently, and somewhat surprisingly, when she and I went out to dinner with our younger daughter, Kelsey. Kelsey had just turned sixteen, but her birth order will always label her as "our baby." She's an extrovert with a capital *E* and provides an enormous amount of fun. For years, another family begged us to let Kelsey go on vacation with them because, in their words, "she supplies all the entertainment." Adding to her status as the youngest, Kelsey is petite — just the other day, as she and I were shopping, she became frustrated when a pair of size zero shorts were too *big*.

"What are you supposed to do?" I asked her. "Look for size negative-one?"

As our little girl started becoming a young woman, she began to attract attention from a number of teenage boys. As a cross-country runner, she's in great shape; even more, she has a marvelously captivating personality and loves God — so it's no surprise that boys would find her company appealing.

I "prayed up" for the dinner, asking God to give me wisdom and the right tone to communicate with Kelsey about this new season in her life; but I felt led by God to begin the dinner by asking Kelsey to speak first. Our daughter opened up a notebook where she had written out, on her own and in her own words, her philosophy for relating to the opposite sex. She began by wisely pointing out the foolishness that many of her friends have fallen into and asserting she wants no part of that. Physical intimacy, she went on to say, doesn't help you get to know anyone, so she stated her desire to never kiss a boy until after she is engaged to be married to him. She further declared her belief that marriage is primarily about giving glory to God, not about one's personal pleasure. She intends to conduct her relationships accordingly.

I glanced at my wife and saw tears filling her eyes. Then I told our daughter, "This is the most impressive conversation I've *ever* had with a sixteen-year-old."

The pleasure my wife and I felt in the face of Kelsey's maturity and character far outweighed the pleasure we take in seeing her laugh and have fun. I suspect the same is true of our heavenly Father. He certainly delights in our laughter and play, but he also takes great pleasure in our obedience.

When I discovered that our older daughter, Allison, for many months had been praying for a family whose father had died, I felt struck with pleasure at the expression of her faithfulness. When so many people (myself included, sadly) "moved on" and forgot about this family's daily and ongoing coping with the loss, my more sensitive daughter kept lifting them up in prayer. I felt ashamed of my callousness and inspired by her faithfulness. I took immense pleasure in her obedience.

Many of us live with an acute sense of how much our sin angers and hurts God; let us not forget how much our obedience pleases him. In speaking of Jesus, the Father says, "This is my Son, whom

I love; with him I am well pleased" (Matthew 3:17). Knowing of God's desire makes life wonderfully simple. We can wake up and ask God, *"What will give you pleasure today?* Would it be enjoying your handiwork with gratitude? Would it be embracing this pleasure as you designed it? Or would you desire for me to ask for someone's forgiveness, implore someone to hold me accountable, or finally lay aside a particular desire of my own?" When our lives become oriented around *his* pleasure, pleasing him becomes our greatest pleasure.

Exalting and legitimizing pleasure doesn't require discounting sacrifice and obedience. In a healthy Christian life, pleasure and obedience always work together as essential elements of being truly human and truly God's treasured children.

Purified Pleasure

Let's make this point practical. A woman who returns to a lonely marriage because she believes it is the right thing to do is motivated by her sense of duty, her love for her children, and obedience to God, not her own pleasure. She may in fact ultimately enjoy a happier life because of her decision, but in that moment, when she must tell her suitor good-bye, she won't believe it; and in the short run, she may have to endure many months of loneliness and difficult relational rebuilding. She may see herself as walking *away* from pleasure, even if she believes she will ultimately build a life of fulfillment.

Sometimes God may call us to a course of action that we believe —initially at least—goes against every sense of enjoyment. At other times, he may clearly forbid what we see as pure delight. In these moments, we must choose what seems like pain rather than pleasure, knowing that, *ultimately*, by faith, it will bring the greatest eternal pleasure.

I like François Fénelon's* take on this: We must "receive" pleasures, he writes, "since it is God who gives them to us for our need." Nevertheless, "we must use them at the moment, like a remedy, without self-satisfaction, without attachment, without possessiveness."⁴ What a practical, helpful analogy! Like all remedies, pleasure has its place. It makes sense to take painkillers when I'm in pain; but taking them after the pain has stopped—and I'm merely hoping for a "buzz"—leads to a foolish addiction.

I trust God as the captain of my soul, and if pleasure takes on an unhealthy role in my life—if I start using the painkillers like an addict instead of like a patient—God will launch a redemptive attack that will reclaim my spirit. Fénelon again: "These gifts ought to be received within us, but they ought not to take such a hold on us that, when God withdraws them, their loss ever troubles us or discourages us."⁵

This trust in God as my Shepherd provides the necessary foundation to walk freely in the land of pleasure. It means that I willingly accept pleasure or pain from the hand of God. The same hand that feeds me and offers me presents may occasionally discipline me. *I must embrace whatever his hand offers.*

For years, however—and this may be true of you as well—I considered only the pain of the cross, not its benefits; and in doing so, I foolishly denied my God much delight. Our heavenly Father loves us! He wants to bless us, his children, with deep and abiding pleasure.

Will you worship him by receiving these gifts and enjoying them, without guilt and with great gratitude?

---

* François Fénelon (1651–1715) was a French bishop and writer. His prominence in the court of Louis XIV helped him anticipate many of the spiritual challenges and temptations inherent in the affluence of our own century. Today he's best known for his classic *Christian Perfection.*

DISCUSSION AND REFLECTION

1. How might the message of Psalm 35:27 ("The LORD be exalted, who delights in the well-being of his servant") affect our understanding of how God views our enjoyment and pleasure?

2. How does a parent's experience of delighting in the pleasure of his or her children reflect on God's attitude toward us?

3. In 2 Timothy 3:4, Paul warns about "lovers of pleasure rather than lovers of God." What are the marks of such a person?

4. The book of Proverbs presents pleasure in two lights: as a trap that can lead to our ruin (14:13; 21:17), or as a gift from God that demonstrates his blessing and favor (10:28). Discuss several ways that Christians can discern whether their pleasure of choice is a trap to be avoided or a blessing to be thankful for.

5. How does viewing God as a Father who enjoys giving us pleasure help us to release those pleasures that are not healthy for us or honoring to him? How, for instance, can we learn to embrace biblical prohibitions with thanksgiving instead of resentment?

Chapter 4

ENJOYING THE EARTH
WITHOUT LOVING THE WORLD

When God gives any man wealth and possessions, and enables him to enjoy them, to accept his lot and be happy in his work—this is a gift of God.... God keeps him occupied with gladness of heart.

Ecclesiastes 5:19–20

He makes us love all that he loves, for his love's sake, and makes us take pleasure in him and all his works.

Julian of Norwich

The world is alive, blinking and clicking, winking at us slyly, inviting us to get up and dance to the music that's been playing since the beginning of time.

Shauna Niequist

Quick question: Do you consider the world a prostitute or a mother?

I'm serious.

Do you see the world God created as a giant temptress, waiting to lure us away from true faith and devotion, or do you see it as a mother who nurtures our faith and disciplines us toward pure devotion and abundant life?

There's a catch behind my question, of course. The Bible presents the world in both lights. Various passages warn about the world's allure, while other passages celebrate its abundance and goodness. The great question is, How do we reconcile these two apparently opposing viewpoints?

Unfortunately, many traditions focus on one to the exclusion of the other. Most often, we choose the negative: the world is a threat, a menace, a temptress. Such traditions deeply suspect any enjoyment in this world and seriously undercut the beauty and goodness of God's creation. They speak as if our job as imprisoned souls is to deny any sensual experience of any kind—and certainly any *pleasurable* sensual experience—lest we lose our appetite for prayer, worship, and Bible study.

Recent traditions of Christianity have had, in my view, a slanted and negative view of the world that injures our souls, opposes abundant life, and dishonors the God who created a wonderful place for us to live. When the biblical writers John and James tell us not to love the world or anything in the world (1 John 2:15–17) and that friendship with the world is hatred toward God (James 4:4), they do not instruct us to despise the sound of a baby's laugh, the taste of cold watermelon on a hot, sunny day, or the drama of achievement. Instead, they warn us not to try to find our happiness, meaning, and fulfillment in social systems, polluted appetites, or actions that antagonize God.

John makes this crystal clear when he defines the world's sinful cravings as lust, boasting, and wayward desires. In other words, these biblical writers condemn *polluted* pleasures. *The problem is that we take the Bible's condemnation of the "world" as condemnation of the "earth."* This serious mistake has unfortunate consequences for our souls and our view of life. Much of the "world" stands against God and rebels against him. God created the earth to reveal himself to us and to provide a place where we can enjoy him.

Only a small step separates hatred of the world in an unbiblical sense and rebellion against God. Satan works with two seemingly contradictory attacks, but both lead to the same place. One track makes us *worship* the created world, putting all of our hopes in pleasures divorced from God. If we follow this path, we will inevitably end up disappointed, ruined, and angry at God because this world can't possibly satisfy us. Depending on the world for satisfaction, wallowing in our disappointment, and then blaming God for our feeling of complete dissatisfaction for choosing an inferior substitute is the path of open, rebellious sinners: "A man's own folly ruins his life, yet his heart rages against the LORD" (Proverbs 19:3).

The other track makes us *hate* the created world, seeing it as nothing but filled with temptation, and thus indirectly makes us despise God because he created the world. Members of this sorry lot suffer a continual sense of defeat. Instead of living in gratitude that God has provided so many things for our enjoyment, these people smolder in resentment, angry at God for putting so many temptations in their path. This failing often characterizes Christians caught in habitual sins, who (often unconsciously) blame God for making the temptations (sex, drink, food, possessions) available. They end up hating the world instead of depending on it.

This latter view of the world can feed the religious temptation to extend hatred of the world to hatred of self. In her book *Neurosis and Human Growth*, renowned psychologist Karen Horney describes self-hatred in a way that accurately pertains to many Christians I have met (including, at times, myself). Horney's markers of "neurotic self-hatred" are "relentless demands on self, merciless self-accusation, self-contempt, self-frustrations, self-tormenting, and self-destruction."[1]

It's easy to sleepwalk mentally through a quote from a book, so let me put these terms in bulleted form and see if any or (God have mercy) all apply to you:

- relentless demands on self
- merciless self-accusation
- self-contempt
- self-frustrations
- self-tormenting
- self-destruction

Do you honestly believe God wants you to live this way? Is this the kind of attitude or life that truly honors God?

Ask yourself some serious questions: Is your "faith," as you've defined it (or as it has been defined for you), keeping you from enjoying life? Are you sometimes your own worst enemy, tearing yourself down, berating yourself, sometimes being unmercifully critical? Do you know what it means to live in the love of God, to know, as David knew, that God delights in you, his servant?

If you place relentless demands on yourself; if, without mercy, you accuse yourself throughout the day for any number of failings and missed opportunities; if you feel contemptuous toward yourself, that you are not worthy of occasionally buying a nice piece of clothing ("What a waste of money!") or ever ordering dessert ("So many calories!"), that you are too despicable to take a moment for yourself, that you have no reason to laugh or play or be touched or served, then you are walking in self-hatred—and this self-hatred will ultimately lead to self-destruction.

A sad and even tragic irony underlies this state of affairs. If in the name of religion we become our own worst enemy, we ultimately become God's enemy, because *God is for us.* To oppose ourselves is, by definition, to become an enemy of the one who is for us. God's grace, forgiveness, love, and mercy provide the only path to true spiritual health. If rules, fear, self-hatred, or obligation motivate you, you will eventually fall—and fall hard.

The contradiction between the world as prostitute and the world as mother resolves itself in the love, acceptance, and mercy of a forgiving God. When God turns my soul toward him, many of the very things that used to lure me away from his presence now become causes of celebration and stimulants of vigorous worship. Where before food might have captured my heart, now it captures only my taste buds and makes my heart sing for such a generous God. Where before acclaim might have captured my soul, now it humbles me and leaves me standing in awe of such a capable God. Where before family might have blinded me to the eternal, now it gives me a picture of what it means to be part of his heavenly kin. While earthly pleasures aren't ends in themselves, they can effectively serve as signposts to God and doorways to gratitude and spiritual intimacy.

Under the self-hatred system, you have no room to enjoy or find new strength in God-given pleasure. What a healthy person would call "taking care of himself," you'll call pampering and self-indulgence, driving yourself until you break down. Instead of thanking God for showing his love by providing you with delicious food for your enjoyment, you'll feel like a glutton if you take the time to actually taste the food. Rather than reveling in the sensual pleasure of getting a massage, the fellowship of playing a round of golf with your buddies, or the relaxation of staying home with your spouse and watching an old movie, you'll despise all these experiences as somehow "beneath" you and as unworthy distractions for someone as important and committed as yourself—after all, you could be saving the world or sitting inside a church.

May I reintroduce you to the wonder of loving the world in a healthy and godly way?

Open Windows

I am bold enough to believe that God created this world not to tempt us but to reveal himself to us. Even this fallen world provides windows through which we may glimpse the one who created it. One writer took stinging aim at a worldview that reduces this world to mechanical chance, devoid of God's mysterious and delightful touch: "The birds sing much more than Darwin permits."[2]

In her wonderful book *Cold Tangerines*, Shauna Niequist

describes how becoming pregnant made her almost mystically alive to the world's truest and purest pleasures:

> One of the best things about being pregnant, I think, is how vividly I taste and feel and smell things. A soft chair can truly make me believe that all is right with the world, and sweet corn and ripe peaches just annihilate me with their flavor. Lavender soap can make me almost pass out with happiness. I have never been so easily and deeply satisfied.[3]

God's design displays utter brilliance. I can't imagine a more intelligent thing for the Creator to do than to make a pregnant mother —who is literally repopulating the world—intoxicated with the beauty of life. If she's going to prepare the way, why not make her an enthusiastic fan?

And yet so many Christian teachers persist in setting God's earth up against God's kingdom—as if the two always oppose one another. We celebrate redemptive activities such as prayer and worship but then pit them against other human realities such as marriage, exercise, traveling, reading for pleasure, and laughter.

Don't get me wrong; the hearts of healthy believers gravitate toward worship, singing, and thanksgiving. All of these good things bring great joy and pleasure. God isn't just our Redeemer, however; he is also our *Creator*. He made us, and he made this world. So when we participate in this world as he made it, we celebrate him every bit as much as we honor him when we do things that reflect his redeeming work. In fact, we insult him when we deny the glory of his creativity. When we speak of God only as Savior, we use him as a rescuer—but he is much more than that! He invites us to truly enjoy him and all that he has made, no longer using God merely to enjoy the world (as he sets us free from addictions, helps us to reclaim our finances, restores our health), but also using the world to enjoy God.

This is a call to embrace the world in a way that may seem radical to many Christians. How can it honor God to ask him to solve our problems, fix our families, and remove the stain of sin while ignoring what he delights to create, color, and fashion? To do so is as foolish as someone learning to play the guitar merely to develop stronger and more nimble fingers, or taking up playing the flute for the sole purpose of improving one's ability to breathe. It misses the beauty and poetry of the entire exercise, reducing this world to a utilitarian throwaway bereft of the mystery and wonder of an infinitely creative and generous God.

I grow weary of the teaching that, even for the redeemed, this good world that God created competes with him instead of points me to him. I tire of the thinking that separates pleasure *from* God; as if I'm supposed to "love" God more than I love engaging in a favorite pastime, such as running or enjoying a bite of chocolate. What a bizarre comparison! The fact is, I enjoy chocolate because God gave me taste buds, and any pleasure I derive from eating it is a pleasure designed and sustained by God.* I can talk about enjoying running or eating chocolate as temptations toward idolatry, or I can talk about them as acts of worship that acknowledge and celebrate the God who makes physical exertion and the eating of chocolate both possible and enjoyable. "To the pure, all things are pure, but to those who are corrupted and do not believe, nothing is pure" (Titus 1:15).

Though this tendency is becoming less common, I'm tired of pastors who seem to always talk down sexual pleasure. God *designed* us for sexual pleasure, and then he gave us brain chemicals and body hormones that make us want to keep going back *again and again*—of course we're interested in sex! God made us that way. Instead of condemning the desire, let's help people build lives seasoned, strengthened, and blessed by *holy* sexual intimacy, seeing

---

*Augustine put it this way: "When you enjoy a man in God, it is God rather than the man whom you enjoy" (*On Christian Doctrine*, bk. 1, ch. 33, p. 28).

it as a wonderful and generous gift from a pleasure-minded and pleasure-giving God.

One contemporary writer sets up this tension between love for God and enjoyment of the world in typical fashion: "But will Jesus be enough? The world seems to offer so much more, so much easier, so much faster. Is there in the beauty of all that Jesus is and offers sufficient joy to keep my soul satisfied and to stem its search for other delights?"[4]

It sounds perilous even to *suggest* that Jesus "isn't enough"; yet the above quote sets up an unnecessary contradiction. How does it dishonor the beauty of Jesus to also seek the delights of art, human fellowship, and God-given joys? Jesus doesn't *stem* these delights; he focuses, sanctifies, and increases them. He created "the best wine ever" for a friend's wedding.* He told his followers to look—really look—at the birds of the air and the flowers of the field. He laughed with his disciples, and he wept when death took a friend away.[5] Redeemed by Jesus, I am finally set free to truly enjoy and participate in the things of this world without becoming sinfully entangled by them.

That, in fact, is the point of these words from Ecclesiastes: "When God gives any man wealth and possessions, and enables him to enjoy them, to accept his lot and be happy in his work—this is a gift of God.... God keeps him occupied with gladness of heart" (5:19–20). Look carefully at what God's inspired Word *really* says: when God gives someone possessions *and enables that person to enjoy them*—this is God's gift.

The ability to truly enjoy food without becoming a glutton, to handle sensual pleasure without becoming its slave, to truly laugh in a healthy way, to manage wealth responsibly and without becom-

---

* It may be worth noting that the seven jars Jesus ordered to be filled with water were containers set apart for religious purification; Jesus took a religious tool and filled it with a creational pleasure.

ing proud or selfish—these are "Creator" blessings *that also require the Redeemer's touch.* When the Bible says God "enables" us to enjoy them, we can fairly assume this enabling to be a second work of grace. Some people who don't honor God may have such things, but not the grace to truly enjoy them. For them, the world may well feel more like a prostitute than a mother.

But not so for the redeemed! Even the reality of our passing lives, the fragile nature of our health, and the ever-present threat of losing such riches will not erase a godly person's enjoyment: "He seldom reflects on the days [or passing brevity] of his life, because God keeps him occupied with gladness of heart" (Ecclesiastes 5:20).

Given all this, doesn't it seem far more profitable to teach the church to thank God for good pleasures rather than to obsessively fear that somehow we must compare and contrast our appreciation for a beautiful painting or a stirring piece of music with our enjoyment of reading through the book of Psalms and meditating on God's loveliness? God wants *both* acts to point us toward him.

To put flesh on this thought, allow me to share a life experience.

A Young Man's Courage

My wife and I have had the joy of raising an amazing young man. Unfortunately, he grew up with his father's sinus system—a wreckage of blocked tubes, pounding headaches, and narrow passageways that regularly get stuffed up.

Even so, this young man chose to be a runner. His drive and his commitment inspired his team. When he was a sophomore, his teammates voted him "Most Inspirational," and as a senior, he shared the "Most Valuable Runner" award. Not bad for a kid who grew up with asthma and has to take an inhaler to every race.

During his junior year, Graham suffered the worst sinus blockage of his life just two days before the district meet that determined which teams would make it to state. I sat with Graham in the emergency room at 2:00 a.m. as he bravely endured the pain of sinuses that seemed so compacted they were going to burst through his skin.

Less than forty-eight hours later, Graham ran against the best harriers in the state. His sickness made him gasp for air, but a close friend was also one of the top cross-country runners in the nation and he didn't want to have to run at state without his team supporting him. As a key member of the squad, Graham couldn't bear to let down his friend or his team.

So he ran.

It wasn't close to his fastest race, but it may have been his toughest. I remember fighting back the tears as he dashed from the starting line at a furious pace. Knowing the pain of a cross-country race, knowing the debilitating effects of a rebellious sinus system, I could only imagine the courage he'd have to show to accept this challenge.

Twelve months later, Graham set a lofty goal for his senior year: he wanted to qualify for the state meet as an individual. That's tough to do in the state of Washington, which, despite its weather, produces some of the most competitive high school runners in the nation. And Graham's district was the fastest in the state.*

We saw him lay the foundation for success. He ran in the rain, even though he felt tired from studying all day, and he ran on the weekends. He faithfully continued his regimen over the summer, even in the hot conditions of a trip to Hawaii. One training jaunt collapsed into the horrific. Late in the evening, cruising through an outlying field in a remote place on Kauai, Graham ran into a swarm of bugs that took on a biblical malice. Like a scene out of a horror

---

* A local boy was ranked fifth nationally in a middle-distance race, but only *second* in my son's *league*. My daughter's team was once ranked sixth in the state but fifth in our district.

movie, the insects covered him like an organic net. Graham tried to wipe them off, but he only managed to smear them all over his body. The black crusaders flew into his nose, crawled into his ears, bit into his eyes, and eagerly marched into his mouth when he cried out against them. He couldn't get them off. I'm not talking about a dozen bugs—thousands of them seemed to stick on Graham's sweaty, glistening body as if he were a prime piece of property.

It took me twenty minutes just to clean Graham's fuel belt and water bottles after he returned. The bug carcasses clung to every crevice.

He woke up early the next day and ran again—though wisely avoiding that field.

Graham has his mother's and my genes, which limits his speed. He has to make up in pain what others have in natural footpace. He worked extremely hard, but his success would rest entirely on his performance on one weekend in late October—the district meet.

I could barely watch, knowing how much he wanted this, knowing how hard he had worked, knowing the level of competition, and knowing that dozens of young men wanted the same thing with the same fervor.

Graham set out with a studious but terrifying pace. He's not a front-runner, so at the first mile, he remained a good dozen spots behind qualifying.

Of course, I began to panic.

But Graham started to move. He picked off the runners one by one. He turned in an incredibly gutsy performance, and by the third mile, it seemed clear he would qualify with ease—far more ease than we had ever dared to dream.

I'll never forget seeing him come out of the woods; I had been counting runners when out popped my son, his face characteristically red, his shirt drenched with sweat, mud caking his shins, but grim determination and noble courage pushing him forward.

"He's going to do it," I said to my wife. "He's going to do it!"

As Graham cruised down the final straightaway, I braced myself for a fall or for others to take advantage of his lack of speed, but Graham actually pulled away from the nearest runners. *No one* would take this from him.

Unashamedly, I wiped the tears from my eyes. In a moment I'll never forget, I looked into my wife's face and we hugged.

He had done it!

I felt so proud of him, so in love with my wife, so satisfied in my soul—a transcendent moment in time. It also provided spiritual benefits on many levels.

Graham enjoyed the pleasure of being fully engaged in life—working hard, being part of a team, sweating, getting dirty, feeling his muscles burn and his lungs scream for more air. For my wife and me, it had a lifelong effect. We have shared something amazing—watching our son, enduring the tension, celebrating the joy—and that pleasure memory will stay with us for the rest of our lives. No other woman will ever share that with me. No other man will ever share that with her. And so we are that much more connected and committed to our family.

Does this love, does this commitment, does this satisfaction, compete with Jesus? Does it threaten my satisfaction in God? Does it in any way weaken true faith?

Scripture would argue precisely the opposite: James writes, "Every good and perfect gift is from above, coming down from the Father" (1:17). Jesus assured his followers, "If you, then, though you are evil, know how to give good gifts to your children, how much more will your Father in heaven give good gifts to those who ask him!" (Matthew 7:11). The only reason my son exists is because God blessed, preserved, and maintained my marriage and then generously allowed my wife and I to conceive and bear children. My son runs only because God has given him a body capable of competing and a soul noble enough to want to. *Everything* about that moment generated gratitude toward God. I couldn't worship him enough afterward.

Some pleasure killers would say, "But would you worship God just as fervently if your son hadn't qualified for state? After all, that's what a *godly* man would do, isn't it?"

To them I would reply, "This moment wasn't about *me* and my response. It's spiritual vandalism to turn one of God's gifts into a test of piety. Can't I just feel overcome by the sheer joy of watching a young man set a goal, work hard, and achieve his aim? Do I have to mar this moment by wondering if my happiness and tears of joy somehow dishonor God because I feel so pleased at the way everything turned out? In fact, Graham's consistent training and riveting race turned me back to God in wholehearted worship. Wouldn't Jesus himself smile and celebrate my son's use of *his* gifts?"

God alone knows my heart, and God alone will be my judge. So what's to be gained by turning an act of great pleasure into a test of my spiritual maturity? Self-obsessed piety can putrefy sacred things when it blows its bad breath on holy moments of pleasure and joy. In the long run, such obsession becomes the enemy of piety, for by fully enjoying and living in such moments, I am less likely to desire impious excitement and stimulation. This day strengthened my family as well as my faith in the God who brought the moment to fruition.

The Jesus behind the Pleasure

And yet, I regularly hear the common questions of guilt-laced piety. Newlyweds ask me if it's possible to love their sweetheart "too much." Young mothers worry that they may love their babies more than they love God. I hear from believers who feel convinced that if they play the piano, God will crush their fingers if it becomes "too important"; or if they're painters, God will strike them blind; or if they're really into their families, God will give them cancer so they'll never see their grandchildren. Businesspeople who work hard to achieve a promotion hear dire warnings not to make their jobs an idol, lest God cast them into unemployment. While most of us don't verbalize these ideas, how often have we thought them?

In many places the church has mastered the art of chasing joy out of virtually every human endeavor.

As just one example, let me explain the spiritual violence we do to young mothers when we shame them for feeling overwhelmed with love for their babies in a way they may not feel *in that particular moment* for God. Neurologists now understand that when a woman nurses her newborn, her brain releases extra doses of oxytocin and prolactin, which are neurochemicals that trigger profound feelings of intimacy and a rush of emotional love. In fact, nursing also triggers the release of oxytocin in the infant. In the God-designed act of nursing, mother and child are all but melding into each other, overcome with intense feelings of adoration, intimacy, and closeness. Their brains ping with positive, pleasurable feedback. Scientists have found this chemical reaction to be so overpowering that mother rats chose their newborns over cocaine!

Our Creator designed this interaction, and brilliantly so. In a season of life that calls this young woman to so much work—changing diapers, struggling through sleep-deprived nights, dealing with incessant crying, breathing in unpleasant smells—it's a mark of God's genius that he also provides for unusually intense emotional bonding.

When this young mother puts down her child and picks up her Bible, there's no way, on a neurological level, that 1 Samuel—and probably not even Song of Songs—can evoke the same release of oxytocin. Making a young mother feel guilty about this—as if something is wrong with her—goes against God's created order. Explaining what's happening from a neurological perspective will help her understand why she feels so close to her child and perhaps not so close to her husband or even her God.

A better response is to teach young mothers to enjoy the intimacy of nursing and use it as a basis for persistent gratitude and worship. Instead of setting up these feelings as something to repent of, the church can urge women to embrace them as one more generous gift from a loving Creator. I can imagine a young mother's prayer: "How good and kind you are, my heavenly Father, that you provide such pleasing intimacy between a mother and her baby. What a joy that my child and I can share these moments as gifts from your hand! You've designed my brain to truly enjoy regular times of intimacy and to bond so very deeply with a child I might otherwise grow to resent."

Let's not vandalize the precious spiritual, emotional, and physical intimacy of nursing, threatening young mothers with the charge of "backsliding" or "falling away" from God when they seem so carried away with love for their child, while (as their hormones settle) perhaps feeling somewhat distant from God.

While we're at it, here's a thought for an entirely different demographic. Instead of responding to a successful businessperson who just earned a nice raise and promotion with a passionate sermon about the dangers of materialism and power, how about telling this man or woman, "Congratulations! Isn't God extraordinarily kind? Let's throw a dinner party and celebrate!"

But couldn't this foster pride?

Possibly, just as *not* responding in this way might foster ingratitude.

If Christians, born of the creator God and redeemed in his image, can't embrace life in all its fullness — the life of family, the life of business, the life of achievement — then who can?

It *is* possible for us to put a person (a child, a romantic attachment, a friend) or a pursuit ahead of God. The Bible presents this as a real threat. We must hold all pleasures with a submissive hand. God makes no secret of how he uses pain, disappointment, difficulty, and dryness to shape us into the image of his Son. Christianity will always sing the song of self-denial. But if we teach redeemed Christians to view feelings of love and achievement as pointing them *to* God instead of competing *with* God, we can use the things of this world to help cement their faith instead of loosen it.

I love the way C. S. Lewis treated a young reader who worried that she loved the Narnia character Aslan more than she loved Jesus. Lewis quite rightly replied that she loved the Jesus in Aslan. Everything that drew her to Aslan was the spirit and character of Jesus, so she didn't really love Aslan more. On the contrary, Aslan merely demonstrated the beauty of Jesus in a way that she could understand.

When a mother loves her baby, she loves maternity as created and celebrated by her heavenly Father. When God our Parent allows us to become parents, we get a glimpse of him. When we love our spouse, we love the way our divine King relates to his people, and we get a glimpse of him in a way that we can understand. That's what we truly love about our spouse. When we love music, we love God's creativity. When we love eating, we love our Lord's generosity and inventiveness. To the redeemed, everything we love about such pure desires reflects on God. We can use these desires to focus our worship rather than see them as competing enemies.

During one of our vacations, I tried to help my kids do precisely this. As we sat around the table, I said, "Everything you like about your life is from God. The fact that your parents are still married—that's our Creator's work. The fact that we have money to go on this vacation—that's Jehovah-Jireh's provision. The fact that I'm able to do what I enjoy for a living, and so have an attitude of joy—that's God's gifting. The fact that you haven't been abused, neglected, or shamed—that's the Lord's discipleship in your parents' lives. Literally every aspect of your life that you find pleasing and satisfying ultimately has its roots in God's goodness."

A Legitimate Threat

Having said all of the above, I need to remind us that we must also see idolatry as a legitimate spiritual concern. Paul warns against those who "worshiped and served created things rather than the Creator" (Romans 1:25). But not worshiping something doesn't mean we must disdain it or even discount it. We can find plenty of geography between worship and disdain.

Let me explain. If I feel distant from God, it is a trap to try to dull the ache with excessive alcohol, risky behavior, or sensual experience. That's a misuse and even a worship of pleasure. By doing so we use the pleasure to run *from* God rather than using it to fall into God's arms. But the fact that I shouldn't *misuse* pleasure is very different from *disdaining* it or pretending that I don't occasionally need it.

Rather than dishonoring God when I find satisfaction in a well-made cup of coffee or a skillfully constructed chair, or when I laugh at a cleverly created piece of humor, I believe I honor and turn *to* him, not away from him. Granted, a nonbeliever can enjoy that same cup of coffee and never connect it to God. He may use that enjoyment as a way to soothe the ache in his soul that is present because God has no part of his conscious, day-to-day life. An atheist can appreciate a well-made chair and never think to honor the Creator who makes our bodies and who gifts some people to work with wood. An agnostic can absolutely make people laugh. Our heavenly Father is kind to the righteous *and* the unrighteous. A day of judgment looms, but God graciously offers moments of pleasure on the roads to heaven *and* to hell.

Becoming alive to Christ allows us to receive and even revel in pleasure in such a way that ordinary things become instruments of worship. Psalm 23 provides the perfect model as David celebrates God's goodness:

> The LORD is my shepherd, I shall not be in want.
>   He makes me lie down in green pastures,
> he leads me beside quiet waters....
>
> You prepare a table before me ...

Wouldn't it sound odd if David had allowed himself to become disturbed by asking, "OK, do I love the green pastures, the quiet waters, and the feasting table more than I love God?" He receives these good pleasures as reflections of God's kindness. Rather than competing with his passion for God, they act as servants of this passion.

When our daughter Kelsey tells me, "Dad, we're out of Special K cereal. Can you buy some more?" I don't reply, "Aren't I enough for you?" It is my pleasure to provide her with a breakfast food that she enjoys. When my daughters were young and I gave them long-wished-for American Girls dolls for Christmas, I didn't expect them to say, "Oh, Daddy, I just love her! But of course I love you more!" I don't feel threatened by their love for or delight in those dolls. On the contrary, I hoped for a response of great excitement. In the same way, God never feels threatened that we delight in his world. He delights in our delight *if we receive that delight* as his kindness, goodness, mercy, and generosity.

We shame singles by making them think it is a sin and idolatrous to desire marriage: "You should be happy in God alone!" But God designed most of us to marry. Acknowledging this desire isn't arrogant rebellion; it's humble surrender to his creative design.

This is why we can enjoy the music, comedy, or artistic creativity of even nonbelievers. When I grow weary on the road and tune in to a Nina Gordon playlist on my iPod, or I'm running with my iPod on shuffle and a favorite David Crowder song comes up, I smile to myself and think how good, how *truly* good, life is, and the only reason I can enjoy such abundant life is because God generously allows me to do so. When somebody skillfully weaves notes together, they take sound as God designed it and send it to our ears—ears that God engineered. Many writers and composers may have secondary glimpses of God's truth, which we can recognize, appreciate, and learn from. Must every chorus say "Praise God" to be acceptable? No—because truth and excellence praise God on their own, affirming him as the genius behind human existence.

The Great Connection

Alberto Salazar, one of America's most accomplished marathoners ever and a devout Roman Catholic, once confessed, "Running isn't simply a discipline, it can become a compulsion—it can become like a god. If you worship this god, you forget everything else. And when you lose this god, you've got nothing."[6] Since we face the very real danger that earthly pleasures can blind us from God and steal our hearts away from him, and that good things *can* become bad things, where do we find the balance?

Listen to this warning Moses gave to the people of Israel:

> Be careful that you do not forget the LORD your God.... Otherwise, when you eat and are satisfied, when you build fine houses and settle down, and when your herds and flocks grow large and your silver and gold increase and all you have is multiplied, then your heart will become proud and you will forget the LORD your God, who brought you out of Egypt, out of the land of slavery.
>
> Deuteronomy 8:11–12

If you take these verses out of context, you could preach a convicting sermon on the "dangers" of pleasure and how it will inevitably steal our hearts away from God. But this teaching has a very important prologue and an equally important epilogue.

The prologue says that pleasures of the world come directly from God's hand:

> The LORD your God is bringing you into a good land—a land with streams and pools of water, with springs flowing in the valleys and hills; a land with wheat and barley, vines and fig trees, pomegranates, olive oil and honey; a land where bread will not be scarce and you will lack nothing; a land where the rocks are iron and you can dig copper out of the hills.
>
> Deuteronomy 8:7–9

A land of pleasure!

If such pleasures would *inevitably* lead us away from God, he wouldn't give them. He recognizes their potential to do that and honestly warns us about the temptation, but he gives advice, before and after, about how to responsibly enjoy pleasure in a way that brings us *to* God instead of pulling us away *from* God.

We find the first step to responsibly embracing these pleasures in verse 6: "Observe the commands of the LORD your God, walking in his ways and revering him."

We embrace pleasures responsibly by *enjoying them according to God's design*—drink, but don't get drunk; eat, but don't fall into gluttony; relish the fruit of the land, but don't get trapped in materialism; enjoy sex, but express sexual pleasure solely within marriage. Any enjoyment of any earthly thing or experience that contradicts God's instructions about how it is to be enjoyed or received becomes idolatry. I can't measure my heart's affections very well, but I *can* measure my actions. No legitimate pleasure contradicts God's revealed will.

Second, we protect pleasure by *acknowledging God*. Moses declares, "When you have eaten and are satisfied, praise the Lord your God for the good land he has given you. Be careful that you do not forget the Lord your God, failing to observe his commands, his laws and his decrees" (Deuteronomy 8:10–11).

In other words, let God's blessings and pleasures *remind you of God* rather than dull you to his presence. The pleasure isn't the problem; the problem is pleasure divorced from God's presence.

> You may say to yourself, "My power and the strength of my hands have produced this wealth for me." But remember the Lord your God, for it is he who gives you the ability to produce wealth....
>
> If you ever forget the Lord your God and follow other gods and worship and bow down to them, I testify against you today that you will surely be destroyed.
>
> Deuteronomy 8:17–19

Without question, there is a real danger in loving the world. In fact, if we consider the *weight* of Scripture, the Bible places more focus on warning people about the allure of illicit pleasure than it does on freely enjoying the good things this world has to offer. Maybe that's because our sinful state makes us so prone to misuse God's pleasures that we need twice the warnings.

But a half-truth is still a deception. God invites us, and indeed commands us, to enjoy this world as God created it—provided we do so *as he designed it*. Under God's law, this created world becomes a lovely place of worship, delight, and spiritual wonder. We honor God when we acknowledge that he is more than a good Savior; he is also a brilliant designer and creator.

⟩⟩⟩ DISCUSSION AND REFLECTION ⟨⟨⟨

1. Growing up, did you view the world primarily as a prostitute or primarily as a mother? How has this affected your walk with God and your attitude toward pleasure?

2. Karen Horney's markers of "neurotic self-hatred" are relentless demands on self, merciless self-accusation, self-contempt, self-frustrations, self-tormenting, and self-destruction. How many of these, if any, do you exhibit or struggle with? What makes Christians in particular so susceptible to these unhealthy attitudes? How might a biblical understanding of grace help us to defeat them?

3. How does remembering that God is our creator as well as our redeemer help us to embrace many of the earth's wholesome pleasures? How does God's role as creator *and* redeemer help us to keep these pleasures in balance?

4. How can Christians determine if we love something more than God? For instance, what would you say to a first-time mom who fears she loves her baby more than she loves God? To a newly engaged person who is concerned he loves his fiancée more than God? To a pianist or painter or athlete who wonders if they love their hobby too much?

5. Gary contends that since God is the creator, Christians can legitimately enjoy the music, comedy, or artistic creativity of even nonbelievers as long as their work isn't inherently offensive to God. Do you believe this to be true? Dangerous? How so?

6. Read Deuteronomy 8:6–20. What guidance does this passage give to Christians about the dangers of pleasure, and how we can receive pleasures without being destroyed by them?

Chapter 5

PARTY LIKE
IT'S BIBLICAL TIME

"Go and enjoy choice food and sweet drinks, and send some to those who have nothing prepared. This day is sacred to our Lord. Do not grieve, for the joy of the LORD is your strength."

Nehemiah 8:10

The battle to resist pleasure and instead do what's right isn't the core battle Christianity introduces into our lives. The core battle is to believe that the Eternal Community of God is a party that we all long to attend and to discover and freely indulge our deepest passions for their kind of fun.

Larry Crabb

I believe that this way of living . . . , this intense concentration not on the news headlines but on the flowers growing in your own garden, the children growing in your own home, this way of living has the potential to open up the heavens, to yield a glittering handful of diamonds where a second ago there was coal.

Shauna Niequist

For Christians who live closely with God, life is like a festival.

Dr. James Houston

Like many teens in the 1970s, I attended more than one "burn your records for Jesus" rally. Some charismatic speakers made a pretty good living traveling the country, organizing meetings at campgrounds, and encouraging us young people to utterly forsake our rock-and-roll music for Jesus, "the Rock that doesn't roll."

As a young, conscientious Christian, I was more than susceptible to this; and to be frank, I'm glad I got rid of some records. (But some, just as fervently, I'd really like to have back.) I spent the better part of a decade listening exclusively to Keith Green, Larry Norman, Randy Stonehill, Kelly Willard, Amy Grant, and their counterparts. Only with tremendous guilt did I allow myself years later to begin listening again to my three favorite "Bs" (Boston, the Beatles, and the Bee Gees).

I can still recall, as a high school student, going through my albums—some of which, had I not burned them, I could probably sell for enough money to put my kids through college—and coming across Chuck Mangione's *Feels So Good*.

"This has gotta go," I said out loud. "The title speaks for itself."

Those of you who remember the brilliance of Mangione's compositions will also remember that Mangione played the flügelhorn. His albums were entirely acoustical, with no words at all. Somehow my guilt-ridden mind felt convinced that a man who would title a song "Feels So Good" must have a hidden demonic spirit in him somewhere, and that this spirit was just waiting to pounce on my soul as soon as I dared to put the album on my turntable.

Why did I feel threatened by a man whose music offered to make me feel good? What in my theology and unformed mind equated "feeling good" with "the devil's music"?

I listened to a lot of sermons in those days. More speakers than I could count railed against a very popular seventies-era poster of a hippopotamus in a mudhole. The caption read "If it feels good, do it!" If pastors had to pay a small royalty every time they denounced a popular poster, Farrah Fawcett would have had more money than Bill Gates, and that hippo would soon be bathing in champagne.

The fact is, I grew up thinking the devil wants me to do whatever feels good and God wants me to deny anything that appeals to me, except, of course, going to church, praying, and reading the Bible. While the Bible *does* speak about self-denial and self-control, as well as mission and service, we go wrong in assuming that play can't be an essential part of our lives.

Our play makes a statement to the world; indeed, it is an act of witness. Far from being a distraction, it loudly proclaims that we, the guilty, have been declared innocent. We, the imprisoned, have been set free. Remaining under condemnation in a spirit of gloom denies the effectiveness of Jesus' sacrifice and his work on the cross, as if we have to make up for Jesus' deficiencies by maintaining overly serious and sober demeanors. Theologian Jürgen Moltmann rightly proclaimed, "Freedom needs more than to be realized, it must be celebrated."[1] In other words, we should embrace our salvation with enthusiastic play (in the midst of an appropriate call to service). If God's redeemed people can't play and celebrate, then who can? Why should such good news make us seem so sad?

To call God anti-pleasure is to dishonor him as the one who created pleasure and who promises us pleasure forevermore. It denies God the glory due his name for paying such a heavy price to remove the weight and consequences of our sin. As Moltmann ably puts it, "Both the laughter of Easter and the sorrow of the cross are alive in liberated men."[2]

Powerless Principles

The problem with the poster that reads "If it feels good, do it" is that its underlying philosophy has birthed much misery and many pleasure-destroying addictions. Feelings *can* lead us astray. Our appetites *may* lead us to ruin. We *do* need to set some boundaries.

But a corresponding challenge threatens us as well: *as Christians, we feel so frightened of the decadence that we often denounce the desire.* The Bible calls this prohibitionist response an unhealthy and unproductive way to handle pleasure. Consider Paul's words to the Colossian believers:

> Since you died with Christ to the basic principles of this world, why, as though you still belonged to it, do you submit to its rules: "Do not handle! Do not taste! Do not touch!"? These are all destined to perish with use, because they are based on human commands and teachings. Such regulations indeed have an appearance of wisdom, with their self-imposed worship, their false humility and their harsh treatment of the body, *but they lack any value in restraining sensual indulgence.*
>
> Colossians 2:20–23, emphasis added

Eugene Petersen's paraphrase (*The Message*) illustrates the message: "So, then, if with Christ you've put all that pretentious and infantile religion behind you, why do you let yourselves be bullied by it? 'Don't touch this! Don't taste that! Don't go near this!' "

John Calvin* scathingly challenged certain expressions of faith that always have to go "one step further" to prove their piety. He points out that the Colossians played the old game of beginning by saying you shouldn't eat a lot of something, so therefore you shouldn't consume *part* of it and therefore shouldn't even taste it; then "at length they make it criminal even to *touch*. In short, when persons have once taken upon them to tyrannize over men's souls, there is no end of new laws being daily added to old ones, and new enactments starting up from time to time."[3]

The church always faces the danger of falling into this trap. Renowned biblical scholar F. F. Bruce puts Paul's words in colloquial language:

---

* John Calvin (1509–1564) was a major French-Swiss leader of the Protestant Reformation, whose *Institutes of the Christian Religion* provided the systematic basis for future generations of Reformed theologians.

"O, I agree that the acceptance of these prohibitions looks very well; it makes a favorable impression on many people and suggests that you have attained a high plane of wisdom from which you can despise the material world. There is something very specious about all this voluntary piety, this self-humiliation, this severity to the body. But does it really get you anywhere? Let me assure you that it does not. The acceptance of all these ascetic restrictions is of no account when it comes to a real struggle against the indulgences of the 'flesh.' "[4]

Another passage reveals that this "going one step further" approach may have spread far in the early church. When writing to Timothy, Paul warns of those who forbid marriage and require abstinence from "certain foods, which God created to be received with thanksgiving by those who believe and who know the truth" (1 Timothy 4:3). However uncomfortable this idea may make some of us feel, it appears that Paul likely sided more with the "permissive" crowd than with the absolute prohibitionists.

In this, he walked in lockstep with Jesus. In his teaching, Jesus never urges us toward asceticism. He never explicitly commands his disciples to fast, for instance. He does suggest that his disciples *will* fast (Mark 2:18–20), and he gives guidelines for fasting in the proper way (Matthew 6:16–18), but these never take the form of a command. Nor does Jesus recommend heroic and lengthy prayer sessions. On the contrary, he tells his disciples, "Do not keep on babbling like pagans, for they think they will be heard because of their many words. Do not be like them, for your Father knows what you need before you ask him" (Matthew 6:7–8). He categorically rejects a strict interpretation of the Sabbath, making the famous and powerful pronouncement, "The Sabbath was made for man, not man for the Sabbath" (Mark 2:27).

Certainly, Jesus at times practiced heroic asceticism—a forty-day fast, early morning prayer, not having a place to call home. At other times, however, he clearly ate and drank in wealthy surroundings (even describing himself as a drinker in Matthew 11:19), to the extent that observers clearly noticed it. Apparently, he also approved of celebratory dancing, mentioning it in a positive sense in Luke 15:25. Jesus assumed his followers would live disciplined lives while warning them away from a testosterone-charged one-upmanship of heroic piety. He wants us to fully engage in life but never to fall captive to it — the ultimate balanced view of pleasures.

As a fan of biographies, I believe the most inspirational and God-honoring lives always walk this balance. They combine a bent toward self-discipline with a healthy appreciation of acceptable pleasures and delight. My theological mentor, the well-studied and enormously well-read Dr. J. I. Packer, vigorously defended his practice of reading mystery novels "just to keep the mind sharp." Theologian Karl Barth, according to his wife, lived a rigorous life of study and self-denial, yet he seasoned this practice with an evening glass of wine or beer while listening to the music of his beloved Mozart. To teach the value of joy, Dr. Barth's confirmation classes typically included snowball fights. On his own, he was a passionate horseman. Martin Luther specifically counseled anxiety-laden souls to visit the alehouse with good friends. And J. R. R. Tolkien once ridiculed C. S. Lewis's choice for Lent — Lewis had decided during one Lenten season that he would drink just two beers a day instead of his customary three!

Without wanting to sound pretentious, I believe God wants the church to reconsider the way we look at pleasure and our prohibitions. Some well-meaning Christians will feel tempted to shut this book and loudly denounce me as soon as I start suggesting that their long-held prohibitions may be cultural more than scriptural. Will you at least pray about opening up your mind to God's truth — even if you have to slay some well-intentioned but perhaps misguided taboos—and prayerfully consider that just because something is wrong in excess doesn't mean it is unhealthy in moderation? What *is* unhealthy, according to Jesus, Paul, and John Calvin, is making an absolute prohibition out of something that God gave for our enjoyment.

Wider Pleasure

As a college student, I read the words of a radical-sounding Christian and popular teacher who questioned why teens would want to do anything other than pray, worship, study the Bible, or share their faith.

"If you don't like doing those things and only those things all day long," this teacher said, "you're going to be very miserable in heaven."

Unfortunately, many believers, like this teacher, define godly "pleasure" so narrowly that they reduce it to specifically religion-oriented worship, which drastically reduces the powerful place of pleasure in their lives. Not only do I think this teacher is wrong about the place and use of pleasure in this life; I think he is entirely wrong about the place and use of pleasure in what we commonly call "the afterlife." It goes far beyond singing worship songs.

In a great gift to God's church, author Randy Alcorn blew away many erroneous assumptions about heaven—including the fact that it's all "spiritual" and devoid of physical pleasures—in his marvelous book titled *Heaven*. Randy forcefully and convincingly challenges the view that all we'll be doing in heaven is praying, singing, and reading the Bible; he calls this error "Christoplatonism," a distortion of the faith that assumes the spiritual is all good and the physical is all bad. Indeed, Randy talks of heaven as having room for pets and even—brace yourself—coffee.[5]

Nineteenth-century writer Henry Drummond* draws great significance from a key passage in Revelation 21:2: "I saw the Holy City, the new Jerusalem, coming down out of heaven from God, prepared as a bride beautifully dressed for her husband." Think of it: heaven is a *city*. What a radical thought!

I'll let Drummond speak at length:

> No other religion which has a Heaven ever had a Heaven like this. The Greek, if he looked forward at all, awaited the Elysian Fields; the Eastern sought Nirvana. All other Heavens have been Gardens, Dreamlands—passivities more or less aimless. Even to the majority among ourselves Heaven is a siesta and not a City....
>
> The Heaven of Christianity is different from all other Heavens, because the religion of Christianity is different from all other religions. Christianity is the religion of Cities. It moves among real things. Its sphere is the street, the market-place, the working-life of the world.[6]

The theological significance of this truth is stunning, not just, as Drummond writes, for what this tells us about heaven, but for what it tells us about God's view of life in the present world:

> City life is human life at its intensest, man in his most real relations....
>
> If Heaven were a siesta, religion might be conceived of as a reverie. If the future life were to be mainly spent in a Temple, the present life might be mainly spent in Church. But if Heaven be a City, the life of those who are going there must be a real life. The man who would enter John's Heaven ... must be a real man.[7]

---

* Henry Drummond (1851 – 1897) was president of the YMCA, as well as being a key leader in the Scottish Free Church. Intellectually astute and spiritually passionate, he played a key role in what became known as the Student Movement, a fervent revival among Europe's youth in the late nineteenth century.

In fact, it's even more shocking than this: there is no "church building" in heaven, only a city! John tells us, "I did not see a temple in the city, because the Lord God Almighty and the Lamb are its temple" (Revelation 21:22). A city, but no church—does that sound like a place divorced from real life as we know it today?

Gnosticism, the ancient teaching that claimed to have "secret knowledge" about Christ, viewed the flesh and the world of creatures as inherently evil. The early church quickly and formally repudiated this teaching. In this heretical view, the flesh was all bad and only the nonmaterial soul was good. This led Gnostics to deny that Jesus actually lived in a material, human body. While the early church formally denounced Gnosticism, Gnostic *tendencies* (particularly the "soul over body" preference) remain to this day. Christians who would feel horrified to suggest that Jesus didn't actually live in a body nevertheless get uncomfortable with the thought of Jesus (and us) enjoying bodily pleasures.

This mind-set has affected how we look at the new heavens and the new earth. In those glorious times, we will enjoy a place of feasting, play, and the arts, including "the best of meats and the finest of wines" (Isaiah 25:6). There will be choice fruits (Revelation 22:2), laughter (Luke 6:21), and the thriving, bustling metropolis of a glorious city (Revelation 21:2). Some faithful believers will live with great riches, which Jesus describes as "treasures" (Matthew 6:19–21). Heaven seems, quite clearly, to be a place of extravagance.

There is no question—absolutely none—that the best, richest, and most rewarding part of heaven will be living in the presence of God—looking on his face, reveling in the light of his glory. That's what he made us for, and that's what will bring us the highest joy. We'll see God in his glory and will know that nothing—no joy, no pleasure, no physical thing—can ever compare. But rather than make us disdain the physical and the peripheral, God's presence will set us free to truly enjoy all that he has made for our benefit.

Redeemed souls need not wait until heaven to begin enjoying these physical wonders. Our time on this earth can be used to learn how to accept such gifts as brilliant evocations from God's mind, increasing our appreciation and awe of his creativity and genius. The Bible clearly celebrates pleasure—but not just in heaven. It has plenty to say about reserving time and money for pleasure here on this earth.

The Tithe That Is Never Taught

Many pastors preach regular series on tithing, including carefully (and selectively) chosen passages from the Old Testament, particularly the one in which Malachi (3:8–9) urges us not to "rob" God of these tithes. But I've never—not once—heard a sermon on tithing that uses Moses' words in Deuteronomy 14:

> Be sure to set aside a tenth of all that your fields produce each year.... Exchange your tithe for silver, and take the silver with you and go to the place the LORD your God will choose. Use the silver to buy whatever you like: cattle, sheep, wine or other fermented drink, or anything you wish. Then you and your household shall eat there in the presence of the LORD your God and rejoice.
>
> Deuteronomy 14:22, 25–26

To be fair, Moses does add, "And do not neglect the Levites" (v. 27; i.e., those in full-time ministry), as well as the disadvantaged (v. 29). But hey—I've never heard a preacher tell the congregation to save even *part* of their tithe and use it to go to an expensive restaurant, order filet mignon and a fine wine, and enjoy this tithe "in the presence of the LORD God," rejoicing in his goodness to us.

Why not? Why do we seem ashamed to admit that God specifically tells his people to use tithe money to feast and even buy an "alcoholic drink" (NLT) or "wine" (ESV)? Do you see how selectively we emphasize certain passages about duty, sacrifice, and obligation while almost completely denying corresponding passages that talk about celebrating, having fun, and even throwing a party? Scripture alone does not condition our view of God and the Christian life. We read Scripture through our cultural lenses. If we take Scripture as it is, we may see that we have become unbalanced in our view of what life in Christ entails.

Pause and consider the implications of this passage: God wants you to use money reserved for *him* to enjoy celebrating with some culinary and liquid luxuries. This does not mean we can stop supporting the work of the church and spend our money frivolously. It doesn't mean we shouldn't give sacrificially. It does mean we can and should acknowledge the role of reverent pleasure, realizing that God created us to enjoy pleasure and that receiving such pleasure is, in God's mind, an act of worship.

This passage in Deuteronomy gains support from another account about the lives and ministries of the great Old Testament men Ezra and Nehemiah. As Ezra read the "lost law," portions of Scripture that had fallen into neglect, people felt struck to the heart: "All the people had been weeping as they listened to the words of the Law." Nehemiah, Ezra, and the Levites quickly determined that the stricken people had given the *wrong* response, and they said to them, "This day is sacred to the LORD your God. Do not mourn or weep" (Nehemiah 8:9).

Instead, they prescribed a party: "Nehemiah said, 'Go and enjoy choice food and sweet drinks, and send some to those who have nothing prepared. This day is sacred to our Lord. Do not grieve, *for the joy of the LORD is your strength*" (8:10, emphasis added).

These powerful and persuasive servants of God essentially said, "Put away the Kleenex; get out the good food and the strong drink. It's time to party." Jesus himself praised the concept of a celebratory party—including music and even dancing—in his parable of the prodigal son (Luke 15:25).

If we had a little more joy in our churches today, we might have a lot more strength.

Of course there is a place for weeping and repentance and sobriety; but clearly, at times, such responses come up short. Some times call for celebrating, rejoicing, dancing, singing, feasting, laughing, and playing.

God's Ground

C. S. Lewis understood all this, perhaps as well as anyone. In Lewis's classic work *The Screwtape Letters*, Screwtape confesses to his protégé demon, "Never forget that when we are dealing with any pleasure in its healthy and normal and satisfying form, we are, in a sense, on the Enemy's ground. I know we have won many a soul through pleasure. All the same, it is His invention, not ours."[8]

Screwtape builds on this comment later in his correspondence, as the master demon admits of God:

> He's a hedonist at heart. All those fasts and vigils and stakes and crosses are only a façade. Or only like foam on the sea shore. Out at sea, out in His sea, there is pleasure, and more pleasure. He makes no secret of it; at His right hand are "pleasures for evermore." ... He has filled His world full of pleasures. There are things for humans to do all day long without His minding in the least—sleeping, washing, eating, drinking, making love, playing, praying, working. Everything has to be *twisted* before it's any use to us.[9]

Jesus gave us a glimpse of what God is like. Despite our insecurities and fears about succumbing to pleasure, we must come to grips with a Jesus who was accused of being a drunkard and a glutton (Luke 7:34) in opposition to the ascetical John the Baptist. In one sense, this characterization badly misses the mark. Remember, Jesus survived a forty-day fast. In another sense, however, it provides a window into the *balance* of Jesus' life. Why would anyone level such a criticism unless Jesus did seem to enjoy his meals and a glass of good wine? Perhaps they misdiagnosed his laughter as intoxication. The one who walked on water certainly never stumbled out of a house, and the one who spoke the world into existence certainly never slurred his speech. Perhaps the Pharisees witnessed Jesus' laughter — he was having a really good time — and this levity led to those scurrilous accusations about drunkenness.

When we embrace pleasure, we stand on God's ground. He uses pleasure to motivate us and to bless us. God tells the Israelites of a great and glorious future: "'In that day each of you will invite his neighbor to sit under his vine and fig tree,' declares the LORD Almighty" (Zechariah 3:10). What gives true pleasure more than a homeowner enjoying his property with his friends?

Those who deny the proper place for pleasure also, perhaps unwittingly, deny the proper place for God. God created this world with some delectable delights. When we open wide our hearts to these delicacies, we open wide our hearts to God. What I'm about to say may seem revolutionary to some and even heretical to others, but here it is: *as Christians, it is our invitation as well as our obligation to cultivate and live lives of true pleasure as a pathway to obedience and even worship.*

══ DISCUSSION AND REFLECTION ══

1. Gary contends that "our play makes a statement to the world; indeed, it is an act of witness." Do you agree? Why or why not?

2. How can Christians achieve the balance suggested by Jürgen Moltmann when he wrote, "Both the laughter of Easter and the sorrow of the cross are alive in liberated men"?

3. Read Colossians 2:16–23. Now read Colossians 3:5–10. Compare and contrast the things that Paul says shouldn't be seen as moral issues (from Colossians 2:16–23) and the things that definitely should be avoided on moral grounds (Colossians 3:5–10). What are some contemporary applications of these distinctions?

4. How is it dangerous for Christians to consistently go "one step further" when it comes to rules and regulations, just to stay on the "safe side"? When is it wise to create reasonable boundaries? How can we determine the difference?

5. How does the reality of heaven, with all its promised pleasures, help Christians learn to embrace (and sometimes discard) pleasures on earth?

6. In a rather controversial section, Gary uses Deuteronomy 14:22–27 to suggest that God is telling the Israelites to spend some of their tithe money on personal pleasure, within a specific context. Is this a fair reading? Is it relevant for Christians today?

7. How do the example and narrative stories of Jesus — including the accusations leveled against him — instruct Christians today on Jesus' attitude toward earthly pleasures?

Chapter 6

PRACTICAL
PLEASURE

Nothing is more materialistic than to despise a pleasure as purely material.

G. K. Chesterton

Contempt for pleasure, so far from arguing superior spirituality, is actually ... the sin of pride. Pleasure is divinely designed to raise our sense of God's goodness, deepen our gratitude to him, and strengthen our hope of richer pleasures to come in the next world.

J. I. Packer

The fire of lust's pleasure must be fought with the fire of God's pleasures. If we try to fight the fire of lust with prohibitions and threats alone—even the terrible warnings of Jesus—we will fail. We must fight it with a massive promise of superior happiness. We must swallow up the little flicker of lust's pleasure with the conflagration of holy satisfaction.

John Piper

Delight yourself in the LORD
  and he will give you the desires of your heart.

Psalm 37:4

Late one night, I woke up to a loud beep.

"Why do the smoke alarm batteries always go bad after bedtime?" I thought. "Can't they ever start beeping in the afternoon?"

At first, I tried to ignore it, but the beep couldn't have timed itself more perfectly. Just before I dropped back into a pleasant slumber, the next beep jolted me awake.

I started to *hate* that beep.

I growled, got out of bed, and went to the garage. Our bedroom has vaulted ceilings, so our smoke alarm is conveniently located twelve feet up in the air. I needed to get a ladder.

I set up the ladder, climbed up to the smoke alarm, changed the battery, and crawled back into bed.

Beeeep.

I must have changed the wrong one!

I threw off the covers and stood in the middle of the room, waiting for the alarm to go off again, just to make sure I knew what to attack next.

It had stopped.

I wrote it off as a technical glitch and climbed back into bed, ready to succumb to slumber.

Beeeep.

My first thought: "Where's Graham's baseball bat?"

I climbed out of bed and waited again, promising to hang in there so that I'd stand right under it when it went off—and that stupid, evil, satanic beep waited until three holidays had passed before it went off again.

And clearly it wasn't coming from our ceiling.

I dragged myself into the hall and saw another smoke alarm. I dutifully trudged downstairs to the kitchen to get another battery and fed my foul enemy with a brand-new source of energy.

Politely waiting until I had once again dived under the covers, the night's pleasant silence ended with yet another beep.

"What's the matter?" my wife asked as I practically turned over the mattress in my haste to get out of bed and rip the roof off our domicile.

"Nothing serious," I answered. "It's just that our house is possessed."

I held my next vigil under the hallway smoke alarm. I could have read the entire Old Testament backward before my villainous enemy went *beeeep.*

Aha! It wasn't that one either!

I rushed into my daughter's room and spotted another smoke alarm, literally no more than six linear feet from the hallway alarm. Who would have guessed? I ripped the unit off the ceiling, jammed in another new battery, and dared, just *dared*, the rest of the alarms to mess with me.

I might have been a wee bit forceful jumping back into bed — my wife found herself catapulted three feet into the air.

"Did you fix it?" she asked.

"I didn't just *fix* it," I replied. "I *conquered* it. I am lord and master of this house."

Beeeep.

"Then what was that?"

The expression on my face — even in the dark — terrified my wife.

"Gary," she said, her intuition from more than twenty years of marriage to me warning her that I was about to blow, "whatever you're thinking of doing, please don't."

I gave her my favorite line from one of the Rocky movies — "I never asked you to stop being a woman; please don't ask me to stop being a man" — and then proceeded to tear off every smoke alarm from every ceiling and throw the whole lot of them downstairs into the garage.

"But what if there's a fire?" my wife inquired.

"So long as the fire takes the alarms with us," I replied, "then God's will be done."

No sooner had I finished speaking than we heard one more *beeeep.*

Lisa laughed.

"You can laugh all you want," I said. "I'm calling in the exorcist tomorrow."

Three cycles of beeps passed until my son came home and knocked on our bedroom door to let us know he had arrived by his curfew.

"How was your evening?" Lisa asked, immediately interrupted by one of the pernicious beeps.

Graham looked at my dresser, picked up my cell phone, and said, "Dad, did you know you missed a call?"

Christians can misdiagnose spiritual illnesses every bit as much as I misdiagnosed that evil beep. So many times, we try to fix the wrong thing, looking for a "spiritual" answer when the solution might be very practically physical.

Marshaling the Power of Pleasure

One of the deepest pieces of spiritual advice I've ever heard came from the pen of the famed nineteenth-century Baptist preacher Charles Spurgeon. "Hundreds of spiritual ills could be solved with a good night of sleep," he wrote.

Spurgeon meant that the answer often isn't "spiritual" at all; it's practical. Do you feel depressed? Tired? Burned-out? Instead of "praying and fasting" for a solution, have you ever considered getting more rest?

Clinical counselor Douglas Weiss gives a marvelous example in his book *The Power of Pleasure*. During his work with a school superintendent who felt depressed and burned-out, Doug realized the guy had almost no pleasure in his life.[1] He lived for work, duty, and responsibility. After talking about his past, they discovered this man had warm memories from his childhood in a rather poor Alabama neighborhood where most of the cars were pretty old and in need of frequent repair. So every evening the men on the block would gather to replace batteries, pull spark plugs, or change brake pads.

This superintendent, stuffed in a building for nine hours a day, overseeing people instead of talking to them about sports and life in general, felt as though he were melting in the midst of his responsibility. He missed regular times of connecting when he didn't always have to make a decision.

He had some simple choices: go on antidepressant medications, quit his job, or learn to build an appropriate amount of pleasure into his already-busy workweek. The superintendent wisely went home and called a cousin who had purchased a car kit the year before but who had barely started working on it. They made a weekly appointment to begin earnestly building the car together.

It was just that easy. The depression lifted, and the superintendent discovered renewed energy. By making a small, once-a-week investment, he became more pleasant at home, more energetic at work, and a much happier person. (This is *not* to call into question a clinically diagnosed case of depression being treated with appropriate medication. Even when medication is necessary, however, lifestyle changes always form a part of recovery.)

Instead of seeking out the latest guru for spiritual advice, I'm calling you to first try something simple: become more intentional about marshaling the power of pleasure in your life. Respecting this God-designed need will ultimately make you healthier, happier, and more effective in your calling and ministry. Denying it for a significant period of time not only puts you at risk but decreases your joy and usually lessens your ability and faithfulness. We become like dull saws, poor imitations of how sharp we *used* to be. More effort won't get the job done; in fact, it'll just make things worse. We need to take the time to get sharpened.

Is your marriage flagging? Well, when did you last have fun together? When did you last put effort into the sexual relationship, or simply spend even a few hours doing something both of you enjoy?

Have you lost touch with your teenager? Why not do something together that makes you laugh? Don't lecture her. Don't counsel her. Don't do anything but enjoy being around her. For just one evening, make it all about fun.

Are your colleagues at work (or church) cutting each other down? Have they been competitive, unproductive, and irresponsible? If you have spent weeks trying to uncover the "buried sin," if you've prayed and fasted for the "spiritual warfare" to lift but nothing has happened, may I suggest a much simpler solution? Do you see any pleasure in anyone's life, or does everyone look pretty close to miserable? Why should you expect a pleasurable climate when miserable people gather together?

My friend Kevin Harney noticed that his staff at Corinth Reformed Church had hit a particularly rough patch due to over-packed schedules, the demands of ministry, and the typical church challenges. With wisdom, he decided to turn an upcoming staff meeting into an ice-cream social. He and the other lead pastor made smoothies, malts, and health shakes (for those who like that sort of thing), and everyone just hung out. In Kevin's words, "We got absolutely nothing done that day except what needed to be done most: we played and ate ice cream like kids." In Kevin's mind, this moment of pleasure became a turning point. "We didn't need another strategy meeting," he said. "What we needed was the sacrament of ice cream and laughter."

For your sake, for God's sake, for your family's sake, for the sake of everyone who has to put up with your self-inflicted state of misery, get some pleasure going! Begin viewing temptation as an indication that your life may have shrunk and that you may need to expand it in a practical, physical sense (while not completely ignoring the spiritual issues). In short, whenever you begin to sense the allure of sin, it's time to find a holy and healthy alternative.

The Religious Trap

Have you ever considered the possibility that Satan wants to keep you from pleasure? Most people think of Satan as tempting us *with* pleasure. He certainly does that, but many times, particularly with certain earnest Christians, he more actively tries to keep us from the true pleasures God has planned for us.

Without pleasure, some of us become angry and tired, feel unappreciated, and then begin to resent others instead of love them. Others of us become judgmental, pointing out the sinful ways of everyone around us (while, perhaps, secretly wishing we could do the same things). Pleasure can be a powerful antidote for these spiritual ills — it can renew and refresh us so that we become more patient, more energized, and more generous with our time and affection. So Satan understandably wants to keep us from true pleasure because he hates its positive effects.

The religious trap that so many earnest believers fall into, however, is that when we get stuck in a sin or temptation, we try to find the religious way out. We think we just need to be more disciplined, more faithful in our devotions, more active in our ministry. There may be an element of truth in this, but if your soul needs true pleasure and Sabbath-style refreshment, and you conclude you need more work, then you're setting yourself up for a train wreck.

And who's most susceptible to this wreck? The most earnest of Christians. Douglas Weiss has observed that it's easier to get overeaters to cut down on their eating than it is to get anorexics to begin eating.[2] We can take pride in our discipline, *even if our discipline makes us spiritually sick.* For some Christians, reserving even five hours a week for something they truly enjoy — be it painting, gardening, or watching a movie—seems selfish, weak, and shameful. If they do finally "give in," they may battle with regret and shame instead of finding rest and relaxation in the activity. Whether the cause is pride, personality, or temptation, they get the same result—the withholding of the spiritual benefits of godly pleasure. Instead of feeling renewed, these poor Christians just feel guilty.

If pleasure becomes painful, if it gets so surrounded by guilt and regret that you can't enjoy it, then you may be under Satan's guns. It's time to take some concerted action. Pleasure enjoyed and cherished is worth fighting for.

If you *aren't* reserving five hours a week for restorative pleasure (we'll get into what this means—and how to achieve it—in the next chapter), then you are likely running on deprivation and are susceptible to any number of spiritual ills. Five hours is an arbitrary number—I'm no therapist—but it seems a reasonable portion in any given week. If anything, five hours a week is probably understating our need for pleasure.

I'm not saying the only reason we sin is that we're spiritually thirsty or bored; we sin because of the residual sin nature within us. We must fight this sin—seriously, intentionally, and untiringly—to our dying day. One of the ways we can fight sin is to build lives of holy pleasure.

In a difficult life episode, author Shauna Niequist discovered the "healing effects of a barbecue."[3] She got lifted out of discouragement by getting together with close friends and eating great food. For you, it might be the healing effects of a solitary round of golf, a long afternoon spent reading a novel straight through, or a morning spent working in the garden. Don't despise these practical helps.

Remember the biblical story of Naaman, commander of the army of the king of Aram? He sought out Elisha, hoping to be cured of his leprosy, and felt deeply offended when Elisha told him to dip into the Jordan River seven times. Fortunately, Naaman had a wise servant, who said, "My father, if the prophet had told you to do some great thing, would you not have done it? How much more, then, when he tells you, 'Wash and be cleansed'!" (2 Kings 5:13).

You may want a mystical cure for your ailing soul when what you really need is a good barbecue.

Disembodied Souls

I'm arguing that we can be more sensitive and perhaps do a better job of helping fellow believers address *legitimate* physical needs — the kind God recognized when he walked intimately with Adam and yet said, "It is not good for the man to be alone" (Genesis 2:18). God didn't say, "Adam, you don't need Eve; you just need to keep looking at me."

If God didn't say that, why do we?

The cavalier "religious" response argues, "Well, *isn't* Jesus enough? Why do you need anything more?" Initially, who dares to argue otherwise? Who wants to say Jesus isn't enough? But perhaps we should question the question. On its face, the definitively true answer to the question, "Is Jesus enough?" is an unqualified yes. But the definitively true answer to the question, "Are bread and water enough to keep me alive?" is also an unqualified yes. Does this mean, then, that I should disdain fruit and meat and even the occasional slice of cake if those foods are available?*

Adam walked with God, enjoyed God, worshiped God, and talked with God — far more intensely and directly than we do today. And yet it was *God* who said, "It is not good for the man to be alone. I will make a helper suitable for him" (Genesis 2:18).

---

* The analogy breaks down here, of course, as Jesus is certainly "cakes and fruits" and not subsistence-level bread and water; but please bear with me so you can understand the point I'm trying to make.

Catch this: God is literally telling Adam, "It is my opinion that the way you are living—just me and you—is not enough, at least not for now. *It isn't good* for you to be here with just me and no companion, so I'm creating someone else, a woman, with whom you can share your life and relate to me."

Brothers and sisters, in one sense *God* told Adam, "I'm not enough." Those aren't *my* words; they're his.

In some lives and in some situations, there will be "only Jesus." God may take away our spouse, our children, our home—seemingly every enjoyment we have. And in those situations, yes, we will find that he is, really and truly, enough. But I believe wisdom teaches us such lives are "invitation only," to be entered into only under God's providence. They are not to be pursued as self-imposed obligations. The early church chastised young believers who sought martyrdom. It's one thing to humbly surrender to ultimate persecution; it's another thing entirely to arrogantly exalt yourself into heroic piety primarily because you want to prove your maturity.

I love François Fénelon's take on this: "Do not anticipate crosses. You would perhaps seek some which God would not want to give you, and which would be incompatible with his plans for you. But embrace unhesitatingly all those which his hand offers you every moment. There is a providence for crosses, as for the necessities of life."[4]

In other words, our Christian duty is to take what God provides and accept his providential provision every bit as much as we must willingly surrender any one particular pleasure (again under his providential care). But let's stop treating falling believers as disembodied souls who need only to become more spiritual. Prayer, worship, Bible study, and fellowship are the bread of the spiritual life, but they are not the only remedies for our ailing souls. Indeed, they become even more effective when joined with other holy "creational" pleasures.

The apostle Paul, for example, told singles struggling with sexual temptation to get married (1 Corinthians 7:9). He didn't chastise them with, "What's the matter with you? Can't you be satisfied in God alone?" On the contrary, he points out that God has made provision for our sexual desires (marriage), and if we don't manage our sexual urges appropriately, we need to more earnestly pursue this practical and holy outlet.

Granted, this fallen world has many disappointments. Pleasures I depend on will ultimately disappoint me, and some will be delayed indefinitely. But just because creational pleasures can't solve all of our problems doesn't mean we should ignore them altogether, as some Christians do. Discovering the biblical place for pleasure releases us to be more creative and intentional about pursuing legitimate pleasure and marshaling its power for the greatest God-honoring spiritual good. I want you to feel free—indeed, to feel *determined*—to cultivate and enjoy soul-filling pleasures that will leave you so full you won't have much time to dwell on the negative or the illicit.

Street-Level Advice

I received a phone call from an associate pastor whose church I had spoken at some years before. He had publicly confessed to the sin of appeasement—popularly known as people pleasing—after failing for a long time to stand up against an injustice in his congregation. Unfortunately, he made a mistake many of us make—one I make so often—the mistake of assuming that acknowledging a sin and repenting of it will make it go away.

That's our pride speaking: "I've seen it, I've confessed it, and now I can forget about it."

If only it were that easy.

A series of events had revealed to him how much he remained

entangled in this sin. When a conflict arose between a friend and a colleague, he didn't want to confront his friend, who was particularly close to his wife, nor did he want to offend the colleague, with whom he had to work. So he languished in indecision and actually made the conflict worse by his failure to provide pastoral oversight and reconciliation. Then his church faced a contentious theological issue that threatened to divide the congregation. This pastor knew he had to come down on one side, but the thought of taking a position that he knew would arouse someone's anger seemed to go against his personal makeup. After a year of struggling with the issue, he still couldn't force himself to face it.

The problem, of course, is that when God calls you into leadership — as God had called this man — "being liked" is a luxury you can't always afford; and this pastor seemed incapable of doing anything that he thought would lead others to dislike him. His sermons made everyone feel good. He was the friendly pastoral teacher whom everyone liked and praised, and he wanted to continue in that role.

Some people would say that merely acknowledging our sin and applying the theological remedy are sufficient. While doing so helps, I believe we can additionally fortify ourselves by looking at the issue more broadly and practically. Without neglecting the spiritual and theological truths (conviction, confession, repentance, trust in God's future grace), we can bolster our lives by addressing what makes us so vulnerable in the first place.

In this instance, I wanted the pastor to consider why he seemed so dependent on finding his satisfaction and fulfillment in his vocation. "If you are living a life of intimacy with God and have many holy pleasures and enjoyments in your day-to-day life, it's not so difficult to go to a workplace and know that you are going to disappoint some people," I explained. "You won't be so desperate for acceptance if you're made strong by a full life outside of that one vocational arena. But if you think you don't matter outside your vocation, if you've neglected your relationship with your wife and kids, if you have no pleasurable pursuits outside the church, then you can't bear to rock the boat at work because work is all you have. Are you addicted to pleasing people because you've let your life become too small?"

By acknowledging my need for pleasure and marshaling it, I can manage common temptations by planning my defense against them. I make pleasure work *for* me instead of against me. I use pleasure to protect my family and integrity instead of to destroy them. Because of my residual sin nature, it doesn't mean I never have fallen or never will fall; it does, however, provide a workable, practical approach to managing the mechanics of temptation.

Putting a "Lock" on Pleasure

Perhaps you're pushing back at this point: "Sure, Gary, I'd like to unleash the power of pleasure, but I'm too poor, too single, too ill, too [fill in the blank]." These excuses only keep you imprisoned.

When I worked in an office and had young kids waiting for me at home, I couldn't get away for long walks in the woods, which I really enjoy, but I regularly slipped out for short twenty-minute walks in a local park during lunchtime. Don't let the impossibility of the ideal keep you from doing *something* constructive.

Douglas Weiss wisely suggests putting a "lock" on our pleasure — that is, protecting it from being the first thing we pass over when life gets busy.[5] If you're the responsible type, you may allow yourself to enjoy pleasure if every chore is done, the house is spotlessly clean, no one within a hundred miles of you is sick, no one needs anything, and the planet has finally achieved world peace.

That's not going to happen. If you're a pastor, someone is always going to need your time. If you're a mom or dad, there will always be uncompleted tasks. If you're running a business, you'll always find more to do. Family won't stop calling, friends will ask for favors, and your church will need you to volunteer — again and again!

If you *always* sacrifice your pleasure and *never* take time to get refreshed, others around you will suffer for it as well. God will have to endure your complaining. Your family will have to endure your attitude. Friends and coworkers will experience the ripple effects of your crabbiness. Your body will suffer the consequences of stress, requiring the care of others. A convicting quote from Elton True-blood regularly challenges me: "The person who is always available isn't worth much when he is available."[6] If I don't take time to recharge, my capacity to minister will nosedive.

Your own neuroses, killjoy people, or your spiritual enemy may try to make you feel guilty for *ever* putting a lock on your necessary times of pleasure, but doing so affirms life, invites you to enjoy God, and becomes an investment in your long-term spiritual, mental, physical, and emotional health. Yes, of course, immediate pleasure sometimes *must* be sacrificed — but not always.

Not always.

Make room in your life for pleasure.

Don't Despise a Cane If You Need One

Ultimately, I believe it comes down to this: Who am I trying to impress? I'm a sinner who stumbles in many ways (James 3:2). My piety will rarely impress a human being, and it will *never* impress God. I live with frequent temptations, skewed desires, a fallen heart, and a soul prone to wander.

Singing worship choruses and studying my Bible frequently sustain me. But God, mindful of my many weaknesses and kindly taking pity on my pathetic piety, has given, is giving, and will give me many other pleasures to fortify my soul, expand my spirit, and enlarge my heart. After a long day of ministry, he lets me laugh at a good comedy, run lazy miles on unfamiliar trails, sit on my hotel bed and shout at an amazing athletic feat on the football field, or spend intimate time with my wife. I believe I would be a fool to reject these helpful friends. It would be the height of folly, the triumph of arrogance, for me to assume I can do without what God has laid at my feet and blessed as good gifts from his gracious hand.

Fénelon takes a very practical view of this:

> The invalid who cannot walk without a cane cannot let anyone take it away from him. He feels his weakness. He fears to fall, and he is right. But he ought not to be upset to see a healthy and strong man who does not need the same support. The healthy man walks more freely without a cane. But he should never be contemptuous of him who cannot do without it.[7]

Maybe you are one of the few who doesn't need other pleasures. As long as you aren't in denial and setting yourself up for a major collapse, good for you. It's not difficult for me to accept that many others have a stronger spiritual constitution than I do. But please don't look down on those of us who know our weaknesses, who believe that, where we stand right now, pleasures constitute not only a gift but a practical source of assistance — a cane we can lean on — to help us walk through a sinful world filled with temptations and trials.

Can I be honest with you? Sometimes those of us who need our canes wish we *didn't*; but when we do need them, we are grateful for them and thank God that he has provided them.

It is better by far for someone to humbly admit their need for a cane and thoughtfully develop healthy, creation-based pleasures that honor God than to pretend they are above such a need and then fall prey to addictive, sinful, and shameful behavior.

Pleasures are to us what a mother's pulse is to a newborn baby.

Since a pregnant woman's heart pulses at an average of 60 beats a minute, an unborn child is surrounded by the steady, sure rhythm of her mother's heart 3,600 times an hour, 86,400 times a day, and 24 million beats throughout the nine months of that child's development. The steady rhythm provides a soothing reality. This explains why wise child care workers have learned to help fussy babies sleep by slipping an alarm clock under the newborn's pillow.[8]

God uses the familiar rhythms of pleasures to soothe our bodies, sprinkle contentment in our souls, and fortify our hearts against temptation. These rhythms allow us to "fall asleep" to many temptations so that we can feel rested and wake up alert for the task at hand. As Dr. James Houston puts it, "We remain human beings with quivering flesh and throbbing nerves who need the small delights of emotional well-being."[9]

Of course, intentionally applying pleasure requires that we know what our pleasures are. This topic deserves a discussion all its own, to which we will now turn our attention.

DISCUSSION AND REFLECTION

1. Do you agree that many Christians often look for a "spiritual" answer to problems that have physical solutions (more sleep, more rest, more enjoyment, etc.)? How so?

2. Is there any area in your life in which ignoring your need for pleasure is putting you in an unsafe or at least unhealthy place, spiritually speaking?

3. Read Genesis 2:18. How is it possible that Adam living without Eve wasn't considered "good"? Since we know that God is sufficient for our needs, how are we to understand this?

4. Think of an ongoing character weakness or sin in your life. Maybe you're impatient or a people pleaser, or perhaps you're dealing with gluttony, sloth, or lust. How can consciously building holy, God-honoring pleasure into your life help you to overcome that sin?

5. Are you one of the Christians Gary talks about who almost always sacrifices their own pleasure for the needs of others? How can you set appropriate boundaries so that you don't burn out or run yourself into the ground, while still living up to the gospel's call to serve God and others?

Chapter 7

WHAT'S YOUR PLEASURE?

*When I wear my favorite shoes on a regular Tuesday, that regular
Tuesday is better.*

Shauna Niequist

*When we see our old personality being changed, then our happiness is
truly a transforming happiness.*

James Houston

*Even the most frivolous amusements will turn into good works, if you
only enter into them with true discretion, and for the sake of following God's plan. How the heart is enlarged, when God opens this way
of simplicity!*

François Fénelon

*You have made known to me the path of life;
    you will fill me with joy in your presence,
    with eternal pleasures at your right hand.*

Psalm 16:11

A legendary account tells of the time renowned Baptist (and cigar-
smoking) pastor Charles Spurgeon invited the famous evangelist
Dwight Moody to preach at his church. Moody proceeded to rail
against the evil and hypocrisy of Christians who smoked. Spurgeon
then got up, facing a congregation who knew him (and his vices)
well, and said to Moody, "Mr. Moody, I'll give up my cigars when
you put down your fork."

Regardless of whether this account is true, two things are beyond dispute: Moody liked to eat, and Spurgeon enjoyed his cigars. A third element is also undeniably true: we naturally preach against someone else's pleasure while blindly adhering to our own.

Let's move for a moment from judgment to humble learning. I'm going to ask you a series of questions that no one in church has probably asked you before, but they are healthy and holy questions.

What gives you true and lasting pleasure? What leaves you feeling refreshed, renewed, revitalized? What inspires you to the point that it inflates your soul and makes you long to be faithful and obedient? What gives you the sensation of a true and satisfying rest?

Is it being outdoors? Watching a classic movie? Receiving a really good massage? Digging in a garden? Taking a half hour to sip a fine port? Letting a 72 percent bittersweet piece of chocolate slowly melt in your mouth? Getting lost in a great novel, perhaps with a cappuccino within arm's reach? Watching your favorite football team, sitting in a deer blind, or spending a cold winter morning on a frozen lake with a fishing pole in your hands? Is it something that makes you laugh, or something that makes you sweat? Is it creating something, planting something, or simply lying on the beach "doing" absolutely nothing?

Have you ever given yourself permission to think about what really brings you pleasure? Or have you felt too guilty to go there?

Sensory Pleasures

Let's take a few moments to look at several of the ways we can enjoy pleasure.

Touching

You may find pleasure in touch, whether it's carving a block of wood or lying down to receive a hot-oil massage. I have a friend who, it's fair to say, has been a bit more financially "comfortable" than us for some time. We met at a hotel once during one of my speaking trips. He had on a bathrobe and was getting ready to receive a rubdown. I've never received a professional massage, but for my friend, who also travels a good deal, massages help him to relax and recover from having been squished inside a plane seat with legroom designed for a three-year-old.

One of the best ways to find out what brings you pleasure is to consider where you spend your money. People who like "touch pleasure" shell out a hundred dollars for high-thread-count, super-deluxe sheets. They consider the feeling of sliding into that soft, caressing cloth worth more than the cost of a month of lattes. Since I sleep in so many hotels (more than one hundred nights a year), I don't think about the sheets much—unless they're awful. My wife and I stayed once at an economy place where the sheets felt like 20-grit sandpaper.

"Oh well," I said. "Maybe it's all about marketing."

"How could this be marketed?" my wife asked.

"Exfoliate while you sleep!"

It almost goes without saying that touch pleasure is the driving force behind sexual enjoyment. God designed sensory delight. It came from his brilliance and highlights the cleverness of his engineering mind. But touch pleasure goes far, far beyond sexual activity. Many women derive great pleasure from the act of nursing their children; others want to get away from their children and soak in a hot bath, surrounded by bubbles. To some, the sensation of swinging slowly in a hammock, or being rocked by gentle waves while lying on the deck of a boat, feels like the closest they'll come to heaven on this side of eternity. Some women enjoy wearing a cashmere scarf wrapped around their neck or bundling up in a warm, cozy sweater. When soft cloth caresses their skin, even a hectic day feels a little better, a bit more endurable.

Hearing

While working on a book with a successful recording artist, I sat in the passenger seat of a luxury SUV. The artist popped in his latest CD — not yet released — and the speakers came alive with sound. The bass sounded deeper and richer than I'd ever heard before. You could feel it, in a good way. But it didn't drown out the harmonies. The high notes sounded distinct and delicate even as the low notes resonated with deep and powerful tones.

"This is why some people spend thousands on a deluxe stereo system," I thought.

And right here we can so easily fall into judgment. Musically speaking, I'm not particularly sophisticated; I'd never understood the dollars someone might spend on a high-end sound system. And the fact that I see *headphones* marketed for $500 completely baffles me. Because I fly so much, I sometimes get upgraded to first class. On one such trip, eight of us (all men) sat in the forward cabin, flying the friendly skies toward Seattle. I looked around in the middle of the flight and laughed. The other seven — everyone but me — all wore Bose headphones, which for businessmen have become the equivalent of a Gucci handbag for fashion-minded women.

For me, that's wasted pleasure. I don't value it. While my pride tempts me to make it a *moral* issue (How can it be responsible to wear headphones that cost as much as some people in Namibia make in an entire year?), it's really about preference. I'd much rather save up to buy a $200 running watch that charts distance and speed, which to someone else might sound outrageous.

Tasting

Every gourmet cook loves three things that I detest: cilantro, garlic, and feta cheese. It goes beyond a mere dislike; I have almost a revulsion toward them. Does that make me sound unsophisticated? When it comes to food tastes, I'm as Joe Lunch-Bucket as they come.

So imagine my "delight" when a friend of ours invited us over to dinner and then showed me what he had on the menu (I'm not making this up). "You're going to love this pizza, Gary," he said, listing several of the ingredients, including — you guessed it — cilantro, garlic, and feta cheese, the unholy trinity of gastric assault.

"Sounds great," I lied, but you know what? He actually pulled it off. It tasted pretty good. That man is amazing.

Lisa thought she had just spent sixty minutes in heaven. I'm a great disappointment to my wife in that to me, eating is primarily a utilitarian function. It often feels more like a chore or a frustrating interruption than a highly pleasurable experience. We've dreamed about one day visiting Europe, but Lisa has made it clear she wants us to go with friends tagging along. "I want to visit those restaurants with someone who can enjoy the food with me," she explains. You see, Lisa can appreciate the taste, texture, and temperature of a well-cooked meal in a way that usually escapes me.

Maybe your taste runs to fine wines or exotic coffees. About 50 percent of the population, including 90 percent who have the capability of giving birth, swoon over dark, rich chocolate.

The psalmist David uses this pleasure sense to proclaim God's goodness: "Taste and see that the LORD is good" (Psalm 34:8). Proverbs likewise celebrates this gift from God: "Eat honey, my son, for it is good; honey from the comb is sweet to your taste" (24:13).

When God promised the Israelites a land flowing with "milk and honey" (Exodus 3:17), he was describing a land that would nurture (milk) and delight (honey). With its gourmet, milk-laden drinks, Starbucks has found a way to deliver both to a modern clientele.

Smelling

In some ways, I have a woman's nose. Women generally have a more sensitive sense of smell than men, but early in life I realized how much pleasure I get from the way something smells. I'd walk by a girl in the high school hallway, be dazzled by how good she smelled, and almost want to propose on the spot.

"Will you marry me?"

"I don't even know you."

"As long as you smell like that, we'll learn to love each other!"

Of course, the way these things work out, I married a woman whose favorite fragrance is "scent free." Ten years into our marriage, I started doing all of my own laundry just so I could get that Tide-fresh smell into my towels and clothes. Lisa uses the organic stuff that, well, smells like the organic stuff I try to wash off my shoes.

I never connected the two, but Lisa has never understood my appreciation for Yankee candles. One time, she actually counted the number of candles I had stashed away and thought about arranging for an intervention; but when I'm working in the morning or reading in the evening, a good candle burning in the background does for me what a quiet classical piece of music does for someone who loves great sounds.

Others prefer the more natural kind of smells, such as freshly cut flowers or freshly baked cookies or pies. Some gardeners crave the fresh air or even the smell of turned dirt. Some coffee aficionados love to drink in the aroma of a gourmet coffee shop. A lot of bibliophiles love to walk into bookstores just to enjoy the "new book" or even "used book" smell. Religious people from more historical traditions learn to treasure the smell of incense, while young moms will tell you that nothing in the world smells as intoxicating as the scent of a freshly bathed baby whose hair has been washed with Johnson's baby shampoo. The Bible celebrates the blessing of myrrh, an ancient perfume given to Jesus at his birth by the Magi and praised throughout Scripture.

If you take pleasure from the way something smells, slow down long enough to sniff. Without embarrassment or shame, add these pleasures to your home and office. Drink in those moments and build a worshipful heart by using your nose.

Looking

Any parent will tell you that few sights provide as much breathtaking beauty as watching your infant sleep, her tiny nostrils slowly expanding with each breath. Your heart can almost hurt with love as you behold such a scene.

When I worked a frustrating job that left us financially strapped, I used to seek refuge with after-work walks around the Manassas, Virginia, battlefield. One fall afternoon, as the sun set over the horizon, highlighting the trees in a truly glorious display of color, I said to myself, "Whether I'm a billionaire or have a negative net worth [as I did back then], I can revel in this just the same." (Of course, the billionaire can *buy* that view out his back window; I had to hike to get to it.)

Looking doesn't bring the same pleasure to everyone, but if it really matters to your spouse, respect it. It makes a huge difference to some people whether they live in a city or look out on a meadow or forest. Others love the beauty of a formal garden, while still others want a body of water that will frame a nightly sunset. On a long day, they may barely hold on until they can spend twenty minutes watching the sun finally dip below the horizon.

A friend of mine toured the National Cathedral in Washington, D.C., with her mother. The mom felt decidedly less than impressed and sneered, "I'd much rather worship in a small wooden hut than in this!"

My friend—a big fan of architecture—responded, "You know,

Mother, you had better get used to this. The description of the new Jerusalem in Revelation sounds a lot more like this cathedral than it does your humble wooden building."

When Lisa and I bought a house some years ago, I didn't understand why Lisa wanted to tear out carpet that was still in good shape, or tear down wallpaper that showed virtually no wear and tear (the house was less than two years old when we bought it). But after we fixed up a room or two, I was impressed by how my wife always gravitated toward those rooms. The reason? They reflected her tastes and thus brought her great pleasure. I thought only of the cost and the utilitarian nature of the house (If it still works, why change it?). My reluctance went beyond stewardship, however. It reflected my lack of empathy, largely because I have less interest in this kind of "looking pleasure" than my wife does. I love nature but feel content to work in a book-lined, messy office indoors.

Pursuit Pleasures

Besides the sensory pleasures, many "pursuit pleasures" describe how we derive enjoyment from what we do.

Creation

Perhaps it should not surprise us that many believers find pleasure in making things; after all, we're made in the image of the creator God. The wild variety of creative arts reflects the enormous diversity of God's people. Your creation of choice can be as intricate as jewelry, as fragrant as candles, or as rough as chainsaw sculptures. Many believers feel most alive when they allow themselves the time to create.

In many ways, our mass-production culture assaults this pleasure. To embrace creative pleasures, we must overcome the crass "legitimization of commerce." Some painters refuse to see themselves as true painters unless they can sell their paintings. Others think they're not *really* photographers unless they market their services or prints. The beauty of being made in the image of the creator God is that we can freely celebrate creating for creating's sake. If you enjoy it, it can even become a form of worship.

So go ahead, make something just because you like to make it — even if you never want to sell it. Go ahead — write the poems, compose the songs, paint the paintings, and weave the tapestries. Make a prophetic statement against a culture that reduces the fine and profound act of creating to a means of economic enhancement. Be a rebel — make something because you consider it beautiful, and because you can.

Excitement

"You want a powerful sermon analogy?" my friend asked.

"Sure."

"While Hurricane Katrina devastated tens of thousands of lives in New Orleans and Mississippi, it gave those of us on the other side of the Gulf Coast some of the best surfing of our lives."

My friend described the adrenaline rush of looking over his shoulder and seeing a fourteen-foot wall of water — "It looks like a mountain," he said — and then riding that wave for a full two minutes (an eternity for surfers who normally get a thrill from a thirty-second trip).

"I'll tell you what," he admitted. "Riding that wave, brushing my fingers through the face of it, knowing the power of that water to crush me or carry me, is the closest I've ever come to that feeling I get from having sex with my wife."

Whether it's bungee jumping or rock climbing, parasailing or skydiving, for some people, danger means fun. Their pleasure comes in large part from an influx of adrenaline. In their minds, if you don't have to sign a waiver warning of possible death or dismemberment, it's not worth doing. Put it this way: guys don't buy Harley-Davidsons to put mufflers on them, and they don't buy Suzuki Hayabusas so they can drive five miles below the speed limit.

I recently passed through a string of three significant injuries in three years—one a year—from training for marathons. My doctor said, "You know, Gary, you're in your midforties now. Maybe it's time to take up a different sport. Have you thought about riding bikes?"

So I switched doctors.

The new guy is a former 2:18 marathoner and understands the drive. His file gets fatter every year.

My wife, after hearing me complain about my primary physician's quite-sensible advice that I stop with the fifty-five-mile weeks, in a very tender, sensitive way asked me, "Well, have you ever thought about running half marathons? They don't beat you up as much."

"*Half* marathons?" I asked incredulously. "You mean, join the people who quit after thirteen miles?"

"Gary, thirteen miles is a long way. Why won't you run them more often?" she pressed.

"Because I don't fear them," I said.

My answer surprised even me. Sometimes we don't understand the root of what gives us pleasure, but that day I realized I have a certain respect for the marathon distance. I can waltz my way through thirteen miles just about any day of the week, but you had better prepare yourself if you plan to make it through mile twenty-six.

Dr. Douglas Weiss talks about the negative effects when men try to "cure" themselves of this adrenaline outlet:

> I've counseled countless men who "used to" do one thing or
> another that met this need before they got married, became

"civilized," had children, and began working a lot. Without realizing it, they eventually lost the risk and excitement in their life. They gradually got in a funk, gained weight, and even became depressed. For many men, risk, excitement, and adventure is a necessary pleasure zone, which (like all others) needs to be managed or scheduled in.[1]

As a therapist, Dr. Weiss has a take that I lack. He counsels risk takers, "Remember that if risk is your primary soul pleasure zone, this is the well from which you drink. It's as satisfying to your soul as any sensory experience you could have."[2]

Of course, while pleasure plays an important role, it should never become our highest motivation. I *don't* think a woman should marry a mountain climber and then try to get him to give it up shortly after the wedding; she knew what she was getting into. On the other hand, when a man takes on a new responsibility, such as becoming a father—particularly if he is the primary breadwinner in the family—he needs to look at the larger picture. Should he risk his family's future in pursuit of his next thrill?

In other words, while I ought to know what truly gives me pleasure, I also need to know my obligations and responsibilities. In certain seasons of life, a person's personal desires must give way to the greater good of those around him. Parenting is one of those seasons. Professional athletes often sign contracts agreeing to avoid risky behavior; fathers of dependent children have even more reason to consider their actions based on their current obligations.

While pleasures are important, they're not *paramount*.

Mental Stimulation

Some couples fight over who gets to fill out the Sunday crossword puzzle. Others like to work on Sudoku or twirl around a Rubik's Cube. I've seen people buy manuals to help them figure out how to "crack" the latest story-based video game. Still others not only play chess, but also read about chess and even watch grandmasters play chess on the Internet. The mental battle of chess represents thrills to them like nothing else.

True readers testify that they find few things as enjoyable as devouring a really good book that has a great plot and characters to care about. They go through the day looking forward to a little downtime, when they can slip back into the author's world and find out what happens. In the same way, nothing feels sadder than finishing such a book—the kind they wish would go on and on and on.

Relationship

Some people just want to—*need* to—connect. Our daughter Kelsey lives to relate. You could call her cell phone the Times Square of technology—always buzzing and always alive. She looks at my lifestyle (working at home in front of a computer, traveling by myself) and cringes at the mere thought of spending even half a day alone, with no one to talk to.

Perhaps you equate being alone with being in agony. You need to look in others' eyes. You need them to open up their hearts and souls. You take great pleasure in socially connecting with others.

Allison, our oldest child, came home from a college ministry meeting one evening and released a very contented sigh. Ally, like me, is an introvert, but even introverts can take great pleasure in social connections. In this instance, Allison, back from college for the summer, talked about how meaningful it felt to worship next to a girlhood friend. "Here we are, in our twenties, still worshiping God." The fact that she worshiped next to someone she had known for twenty of her twenty-one years made it all the more pleasurable.

Biblical counselor David Powlison says it so well: "Paradise itself is living in the presence of the Person you most enjoy, in a room full of people with whom you are perfectly at ease, whom you are delighted to see."[3]

If you're a stay-at-home parent and you find your pleasure zone in interacting with others, you have to find ways to connect. Finances may dictate that you relate to friends while still watching the kids, but you owe it to yourself and to those around you to address this need. If you suffer in your loneliness all day long and then expect a tired spouse to come home and feel eager to talk, listen, and relate — after he or she has done those things all day at the office — then you're setting yourself up for frustration.

Before we leave this topic, a word to the tired spouse: If your wife feels lonely and you consistently deny her the pleasure of relating and speaking intimately to you, you're being very foolish. To know that your spouse takes great pleasure in relating and then to not even make an attempt to give her moments of that pleasure borders on cruelty. If she's extremely relational, you may never be able to meet all of her conversational needs. But to refuse to try to meet *some* of them is inexcusable. It's like a woman marrying a golfer or a hunter and then asking him never to golf or hunt again. If you're relational toward your wife to get her to marry you but then emotionally check out of the relationship after the wedding, you've committed fraud. A highly relationally oriented woman will happily make other friends as well, but even if she has half a dozen close girlfriends, she'll still *always* want to have an intimate relationship with her husband. That's a legitimate, even holy, desire.

Laughter

Laughter has stunning physiological effects. Taking in a good joke is to the soul what eating a healthy salad with low-fat protein is to the body — about as nourishing as it gets.

Sharing laughter with someone else is one of life's great pleasures. While teaching a seminary class, I mentioned the television show *The Office* in an offhand way. About a dozen students started laughing, without me saying anything more. There's just something about Michael's stupidity, Dwight's bizarreness, Stanley's insufferability, and Toby's endurance of his narcissistic, idiot boss's hatred that gives some of us sheer delight. Just the mention of the show makes us laugh.

For those needing a laughter fix, satellite radio makes comedy as accessible as music, while cable television brings stand-up into our homes twenty-four hours a day. I've never laughed harder, however, than when children surround me in real-life situations. And these situations require far less discernment than media-based comedy, which is often more inappropriate than spiritually healthy.

We can also gain something from having a good laugh at church at the end of a long week. I know some people consider laughter in a worship service suspect at best, but we'll discuss this notion more thoroughly in a later chapter.

Putting Pleasure into Play

You've probably identified other pleasures we haven't addressed: Travel, for instance, is a big one for many. Volunteering. Politics and the drama of elections. Hunting and golf.* I can't give you an exhaustive list, but I do want to get you thinking about legitimate activities that often make many Christians feel guilty. What gives you true and lasting pleasure? Within your current schedule, how can you begin opening the door to experience some of these delights?

In church, you often get asked, "How much time every day do you spend in prayer? Are you reading the Bible every day? When did you last share your faith with a nonbeliever? For which ministry of the church will you volunteer your time to help it succeed?"

---

* Douglas Weiss deals with many of these in his book *The Power of Pleasure*.

A place exists for these questions. To be honest, studying and spending time in prayer are two of my *greatest* pleasures. But I consider it dishonest when the church presents these activities as the *only* pleasures, as though God accepts only purely "religious" activities. That's why I purposefully *didn't* list what Douglas Weiss in his book calls the "spirit pleasures." Millions of trees have given their lives to scold Christians about the importance of meditating, praying, serving, giving, and the like—and thank God for this. But it's time we evangelicals gave ourselves permission to sip a cup of coffee, watch an afternoon ball game, or light a Yankee candle without feeling as though God has to excuse himself from the room. Why not rather think of him as the ultimate author of that pleasure?

Build your life by making room for healthy pleasures that lift your soul in the midst of often difficult days. Maybe sitting in a local coffee shop for fifteen minutes a day is the only "vacation" you'll get. Maybe it'll take you three days to watch a two-hour movie featuring Humphrey Bogart or Tom Hanks. Perhaps you have to settle for just three runs a week, listening to Mozart on your iPod in ten-minute increments, or putting off that conversation until 10:00 p.m., when the kids finally climb into bed—but find a way to squeeze in these soul-building pleasures.

Be honest about your desires and realistic about your ability to live with frustration. Has denying your soul left you vulnerable to deceit and illusion? Have you put your integrity, ministry, and family in jeopardy by living as though you can go 24-7 without a break, without any fun, without any true pleasure? If you're trying to do so—if you think you can ignore the place of pleasure in your life—then I believe you're being naive, particularly since you live in the twenty-first century.

⟩⟩⟩ DISCUSSION AND REFLECTION ⟨⟨⟨

1. Reread the first few paragraphs of this chapter detailing the story of Spurgeon and Moody. Why do you think we are so blinded to the danger of our own preferred pleasures and so acutely aware of the danger of others' preferred pleasures? How can we be more honest about our own enjoyment and more understanding of others'?

2. List the five sensory pleasures—touch, sound, taste, sight, and hearing—in the order of their importance when it comes to what gives *you* the most pleasure. Do this for your spouse (or a friend) as well. Now trade lists, and see how well you know each other.

3. Which one of the pursuit pleasures consistently gives you lasting enjoyment?

4. Can you think of any other personal pleasures? If so, share them.

5. Does your life contain enough of these pleasures, or too much?

Chapter 8

SPIRITUAL FERNS

What do we need?... Not to neglect our own needs while devoting ourselves to those of others, and not to neglect the needs of others while being engrossed in our own.

François Fénelon

It was like I didn't really know how bad I felt until I started feeling good.

Alberto Salazar

They feast on the abundance of your house;
  you give them drink from your river of delights.

Psalm 36:8

"See this fern?" Our tour guide's firm voice sounded full of foreboding. "It's the most dangerous plant in all of Hawaii."

Everyone took a step back.

Poison doesn't make this particular fern so dangerous, as everyone who stepped back anticipated. Its peril lies in something far more indirect. Our guide explained, "This fern grows only on really steep inclines. You're standing right next to a direct vertical drop, but the fern gives you a false sense of a gentle slope, so people step on it and tumble to their deaths."

Some "spiritual ferns" are just as deadly. On their own, they won't kill you; but they signal that you're walking next to a treacherous cliff. I've identified at least three, all related to our view of pleasure. Maybe you can name others.

Tiredness

I didn't recognize the spiritual power of pleasure without a struggle. In fact, recently it dawned on me that I had been running an unwise schedule *for a couple of years.* Finally, during a two-week vacation — the first I had taken in quite some time — God slowed me down long enough to help me look at my life objectively. The honesty of that look astonished and terrified me. Had I been my own spiritual director, I would have said, "Gary, by living your life the way you are, you are choosing one of three things: a heart attack, a nervous breakdown, or an affair."

By living only out of obligation, neglecting our need for rest and recreation, we ultimately *choose* a spiritual breakdown. We don't think we're choosing a spiritual breakdown, but all of our little choices set us up for precisely that.

Here's where well-meaning Christians can get themselves into serious trouble. Our pride leads us to believe that we can set unhealthy schedules and not suffer the consequences. This isn't faith; it's neurosis.

Many of us actually take pride in our drivenness. Psychoanalyst Karen Horney makes this comment: "If we tell a patient that he expects too much of himself, he will often recognize it without hesitation.... He will usually add, explicitly or implicitly, that it is better to expect too much of himself than too little."[1]

So an earnest college student goes away to a challenging university, living on caffeine and five hours of sleep a night, and slowly loses his joy. He then finds himself drifting from prayer, and eventually he wakes up having spent an evening doing things that would have appalled him in an earlier life. And yet he is actually surprised: "How did *that* happen?"

A young mother pushes herself—acting heroically, balancing work and family life, denying basic needs such as sleep, rest, good nutrition, and an occasional break from screaming toddlers with runny noses—and then feels surprised when she discovers she has "fallen out of love" with her husband or realizes she has a tendency to "get a little rough" with one of her kids.

A well-meaning elder or deacon sacrifices for his vocation, sacrifices for his wife, sacrifices for his kids, and gives up many evenings sacrificing for his church—and then is astounded when his body breaks down or he has a spiritual meltdown and collapses into an affair or develops an addiction. As Karen Horney observes, "His demands that limitations in time and energies should not exist for him are stronger than reason."[2]

Dr. Patrick Carnes, one of the foremost experts on sexual addiction, sees pleasure relaxation and leisure as essential elements to break the cycle and power of addictions:

> Almost all relapse from any addiction starts with life-style imbalance. Living in the extremes—being frenetic, overextended, and depleted—leads to addictive feelings of entitlement (I deserve it) and denial (just a little will not matter). The rewards of relationship and the serenity of recovery will remain elusive under those circumstances. Put simply: addicts and co-addicts often do not know how to play or enjoy themselves. For many, stopping to smell the roses feels awkward, undeserved, and unproductive.[3]

"Religious addicts" also need to be wary. Many times I have fallen into the trap of assuming the most difficult thing for me is always God's will. Anything pleasant or fun, by definition, borders on "compromise." No less a light than François Fénelon helped me to see the danger in this line of thinking: "Nothing is more false and more indiscreet than always to want to choose what mortifies us in everything. By this rule a person would soon ruin his health, his business, his reputation, his relations with his relatives and friends, in fact, every good work, which Providence gives him."[4]

Let's say you have a vacation planned (or maybe just a weekend off) and someone calls with an "urgent" need. Do you always assume the "godly" thing to do is to give up your weekend and go meet that need? Perhaps God has given you a heart to take in foster children; be careful that you don't overload your marriage, taking away legitimate time to keep connecting as a couple. If your spiritual enemy can't get you to apply the brakes to keep you from ministering, he may well try to get you to push the gas pedal to the floor, hoping to drive you off a cliff.

At this point, pride becomes especially dangerous. Masquerading as spiritual maturity, pride tells us that we're unusually strong, or at least we've received a special anointing through which we can break the rules and yet not fall. We may think we don't need the occasional times of rest and pleasure that the "weak" need, and we may even spiritualize our breaking of the rules by calling it "faith." But you know what? The rules *do* apply to us. If I eat 5,000 calories a day and don't exercise, I'm going to become obese—and I will die sooner rather than later. If I ignore my marriage, my wife and I will drift apart. It doesn't matter whether I ignore my marriage to prepare a sermon, homeschool a child, teach a Bible study, or lower my golf handicap. If I ignore my marriage, we'll drift, and we'll become more vulnerable to an affair or a divorce. If I don't rest, if I expect my body to keep pushing, eventually it'll break down.

We need to humbly recognize that God made us in such a way that we have a need for real, true, and lasting pleasure. If we deny this need, pretend it doesn't exist, and keep driving ourselves into the ground, ultimately our psyches will rebel, and we'll become another sad example of someone who had a decent start but a deplorable finish.

You are no different from anyone else. *If you push yourself too hard, if you deny yourself legitimate pleasure, if you allow your life to become only about duty, responsibility, and obligation, then eventually you will have a spiritual meltdown, a mental collapse, or an emotional breakdown.*

Our lives may not allow us to enjoy minivacations and innocent pleasures as often as we would like, but to deny them altogether sets us up for failure and robs God of the pleasure he takes in our own enjoyment.

Please listen to me, for your own sake: *The rules apply to you.* You are not superhuman. God designed you with certain needs—including rest, sleep, nutrition, and relaxation—and even commands a regular time of slowing down (the Sabbath). If you ignore reason and God's commands, you will suffer painful consequences. They may not come immediately, but they will come. Only arrogance and denial, not faith, tell you to ruthlessly run yourself into the ground and expect that your soul won't ultimately break down or rebel.

Consider tiredness a "spiritual fern." We need to respect its warning signs and understand how it sets us up for a potential fall.

Loneliness/Alienation

A Trinitarian God designed us to live in community and relationship. And so it is worth struggling for connectedness and intimacy. Without it, we risk any number of personal and spiritual ills. As one writer puts it, "The clergy are often very lonely, and a great many disastrous things occur in life because of loneliness."[5]

Both introverts and extroverts need to connect with others. The *amount* of time you prefer to spend in other people's presence and the *way* you spend that time (talking about trivial things, laughing at jokes, or deeply connecting through sharing) may differ, but God created all of us as social beings. After creating Adam, God said, "It is not good for the man to be alone" (Genesis 2:18).

We are best off tending social interaction something like a garden. Because we live in a social world, we'll "fall" into relationships of various kinds, but the wise person intentionally manages this pursuit. One study found that happiness "is more closely related to *social interaction* than to any other environmental control."[6] Deep, abiding pleasure — the kind that lasts — has a relational component. God didn't make us so that we would isolate ourselves. Our social connections radically influence our sense of well-being.

Have you ever noticed how sin isolates us? The Bible tells us not to give up meeting together (Hebrews 10:25), but most sins seem designed to get us to do exactly this. A man once told me one of the saddest stories I've ever heard. He confessed that, due to a propensity to visit unsavory sites on the Internet, he felt more and more isolated from his family. In fact, one time while trolling for images online, he heard the front door open and his wife and kids walk into the house. He actually felt *disappointed* that they had come home. As a father experiencing the emotions of seeing my kids leaving for college, I ache at the thought of cultivating a habit that would make me *regret* having my family walk through the door.

But every sin does this. People who gorge themselves on food admit to hiding their stash and slipping away into a side room or closet to consume an entire carton of ice cream — always by themselves. Alcoholics often don't recognize their addiction until they realize how much they hide from people when they drink. Men and women engaged in an affair don't hang around the neighborhood — they find places to go where no one will recognize them.

Whenever I find myself in isolation, whenever I regret being around loved ones, whenever I am hiding, I'm right next to a *spiri-*

tual fern, a sign that I'm getting into an unhealthy situation, habit, or lifestyle. As an introvert, I understand the need to spend time in solitude, but there's a big difference between "processing" and "hiding."

This may sound contradictory, but the need to develop social interaction pertains *especially* to couples. You can isolate yourself as a pair, or even as a family. Couples who do this in the infatuation stage risk losing the friends they'll need when the infatuation fades or when the couple begins to contemplate marriage. They lose the perspective of older and wiser couples just when they need it most, and they may cement a relationship in marriage that objective friends could have warned them about. A healthy relationship breeds broader social interaction; isolation is, by definition, an unhealthy by-product of an unhealthy relationship.

The danger of "couple isolation" remains even after the marital commitment. Without cultivating community, during those times when your marriage goes through the inevitable challenges and seasonal distances, you'll lack the support of God's church to prop you up. My wife and I have witnessed many couples on the verge of collapse, barely hanging on in their marriage. Virtually without fail, the ones who made it through and now enjoy a contented marriage joined a small group that enfolded the couple with prayer and friendship.

Think of getting involved in a small group as buying "marriage insurance." You can go years without actually needing car insurance, but you keep making the payments because you know, in a world like this one, you'll probably have an accident at one time or another. The same thing happens relationally. You may cruise through a couple of decades, but when this world starts to tear you apart—as it tries to do with virtually every couple—you need some support. Don't isolate yourself as a family. Become an active, engaged part of your local church.

If, as an individual or as a couple, you live a lonely life, you walk near the spiritual edge. If you walk near the edge for a long time, eventually you'll fall off. God didn't design you as a hermit, either emotionally or socially. We have to take the time, push past the hurt, make the effort, and endure the occasional pain and disappointment to engage in the holy pleasure of social interaction. Relating to others is like exercise; we may not always feel like doing it, but if we allow our reluctance to rule our response every time, we'll become very unfit—and personally, very unhappy.

Lack of Joy in Life and in God

Recent brain research provides many insights into how our minds and emotions work. We now know, for instance, that, neurologically speaking, happiness can be acquired, managed, and largely explained through the brain chemicals that course through our bodies. Exercise, which releases endorphins, contributes to this sense, as do creative endeavors and sexual intimacy (which releases oxytocin). Laughter spawns all sorts of positive chemical reactions. Even something as simple as warm, swirling water (hot tubs) can release endorphins.

Wisdom and even obligation suggest we must be intentional about these physical and personal realities. Surly, frustrated saints don't serve God well. When I lack joy in life, or when daily existence becomes mere drudgery, I become a walking time bomb. If someone criticizes me, I will likely respond in anything but a godly way. If someone disappoints me or sins against me, my living a dreary, disappointed life makes it very unlikely that I will respond in a way that reflects the character of Christ.

But when I intentionally pursue holy and good pleasure, it amazes me how much more patient and understanding I can become. When someone criticizes me unfairly, I can actually feel sorry for their insecurity or misery rather than vengeful about the hurt they inflict.

Occasional mood swings happen. I'm not talking about always walking around with a silly grin. But if you know Jesus and still have been dour and grumpy for a long season, if you can't remember the last time you laughed, if you feel like you're ready to explode, then (though in and of itself that state may not technically be "sinful") sin may be crouching at your door, just waiting for the right opportunity to strike. It will find you out, sooner rather than later. You need to treat this state as a spiritual fern, a sign of danger, and take appropriate action.

When you cultivate a devotional life built on delight, you find one of the best ways to combat this grumpiness. I wrote *Sacred Pathways* (which insists that God created all of us with different spiritual temperaments or "pathways") to teach this very truth. Understanding how we best connect with God will help us create nourishing and consistent times with him. When we turn our daily time with God into an obligation, we risk emptying it of much of its restorative power.

There will always be a place for discipline. I don't spend concentrated time with God *only* when I feel like it, but when I design a devotional time that I enjoy, I almost always *do* feel like it. I've had a lifelong love affair with the Christian classics, and few things touch my heart like reading the words of ancient wisdom, passed down and applied by the Holy Spirit to my contemporary life. If you're a contemplative, an enthusiast, a caregiver, an activist, or one of the other five temperaments, you'll want to build on different types of devotional activities than the one I build on, so it helps to know your temperament.

When I walk closely with God, cultivating and protecting time with him, I simply love people a whole lot more. One time, after a particularly rich weekend of ministry, I sat on an airplane practically *bursting* with the desire to love and bless as many people as possible. I started praying, "Lord, who can I encourage? Who can I bless? Who can I serve?" This opened the door to such joy that I can't imagine thinking it would feel "pleasurable" to intentionally hurt, corrupt, cheat, or exploit.

As sinful people with sin-filled hearts, we can't expect to maintain hearts of love, generosity, and service on our own. Let's learn to delight in God so that we can delight in others and even delight in life.

Remember, drudgery, a dour attitude, and a tension-filled spirit all warn that we may be headed for a fall if we don't turn around.

It's the Second Injury That'll Stop You

Seasoned runners will tell you it's not the first injury that will sideline you, but the second. You can often run through a minor injury. But if you do it too aggressively, you set yourself up for a major injury once your body begins to compensate.

While training for one marathon, I developed a slight case of bursitis in my right hip. Bursitis feels uncomfortable, marked by a dull burning sensation, but you can easily manage the pain. Within about a month of entering my taper,* I ignored it—until I woke up one morning with the inside of my right knee on fire.

I've heard it so many times: Someone has a sore hamstring but keeps training and then wakes up with an enflamed Achilles tendon. Someone has tight quadriceps, imperceptibly changes her gait, and ends up with a stress fracture in her foot. Our bodies *will* compensate. Minor injuries, if ignored, commonly lead to much bigger and more serious injuries.

The same thing happens with our souls. Feeling down and a

---

* A period of reduced mileage before a race, usually two to three weeks before a marathon.

little grumpy may not be, on its own, a sin, but it often leads us to respond to events in a sinful way. Alienation, while not a scandal, can tempt us to wade into scandalous waters. Tiredness, while not a spiritual failing, can set us up for a serious fall.

If you ignore the loneliness, the alienation, the tiredness, you can function quite well—for a while. But sooner or later, as surely as Christmas comes near the end of December, you'll find yourself struggling with a much bigger problem. Your soul will compensate. "If you won't take time for pleasure," it will say, "I'll find my own. If you won't plan for rest, if you keep pushing me this hard, I'm going to crave an entirely different form of rest. If you won't cultivate real intimacy, I'll find a false intimacy."

Not cultivating a healthy, soul-restoring hobby will not keep you out of heaven, but one day you may stumble across something on the Internet, or feel drawn into the illicit thrill of gambling, or find something else that suddenly provides a much-needed "break" from the stresses and strains of life and ministry.

Most of us don't have enough self-awareness to notice these minor points of compensation until they become problems. We miss the process and wake up with the destruction. We then try to manage the destruction but completely ignore the process that led to the destruction. That launches us into a life of avoidance— treating the symptoms without ever curing the disease.

When we respect the spiritual power of pleasure, we can learn to manage our lives before the tiredness, loneliness, or drudgery (all of which occur occasionally in a hurried, fallen world) reaches dangerous levels. My wife and I have never had the luxury of owning a hot tub, but we've talked to many couples who testify to the pleasure and corresponding power of a twosome spending four or five nights a week soaking in hot water, talking about their day, reconnecting with each other, relaxing their bodies, and releasing endorphins that put them in a better mood. Others might prefer a nightly drink out on the patio, a joint trip to the health club, or something else. These simple rituals humbly recognize that our souls need a certain amount of pleasure, human connection, and joy to function in a healthy manner.

I've found that if something doesn't become routine, it usually dies. A couple never plans to drift apart; they just "forget" to keep reconnecting. The same principle explains why I appreciate running so much. Five days a week, I get to enjoy this restorative routine, this minivacation. I know that when I wake up, I'm going to spend some time in the Word. And five days out of seven, I'm going to lace up my shoes, get outside, and spend some time on the trails. To you that may sound like torture, not pleasure. But here's the bottom line: be sure to find your own restorative routine—before the lack of one knocks you down.

I pray that you will use the "spiritual ferns" model as a warning to take a step back. Ask yourself these three questions:

Am I consistently tired?

Do I feel really lonely?

Am I living, worshiping, and ministering out of a sense of joy and delight in the Lord, or do I feel driven by frustration, duty, and obligation?

If any one of these proves problematic for you, be careful. You're entering the danger zone. If two resonate, you're teetering on the edge and should make some major changes in your life *right now*. If all three characterize your life, may I suggest you visit someone *today* who can provide pastoral care and help put you back on a solid path?

The stakes are high, and the battle is real. Let's take the "spiritual ferns" seriously. Let's help each other learn how to diagnose spiritual ills before they become spiritual disasters.

DISCUSSION AND REFLECTION

1. On a scale of one to ten, how tired are you? Not just today (you may not have slept well last night), but over the course of the last several months, would you say you're rested and refreshed, or close to running on fumes?

2. Gary writes, "If you push yourself too hard, if you deny yourself legitimate pleasure, if you allow your life to become only about duty, responsibility, and obligation, then eventually you will have a spiritual meltdown, a mental collapse, or an emotional breakdown." Do you think this is true? If so, why do so many Christians put themselves in such danger? Why do we think overwork, with little to no play, is a virtue instead of a vice?

3. On a scale of one to ten, how lonely are you personally? If you're married or dating, how lonely are you as a couple? What changes can you make in the coming weeks to address any weaknesses in this area?

4. On a scale of one to ten, how filled with joy are you? What has contributed to this abundance (or lack thereof)?

5. Do you feel like you're "compensating" for any personal weakness at this point in your life? How can you address the original issue so that you don't fall into an unhealthy pattern of behavior?

6. Can you name any other "spiritual ferns" that Gary doesn't mention?

Chapter 9

PRESERVING PLEASURE

I agree that pleasure as such is good, but not that all pleasant things are good.

Peter Kreeft

Sin can only live in the heart that does not love goodness with all its strength. Only a feebleness of desire for God enables sin to be a tyrant. It will disappear as though it had never been immediately one craves for righteousness wholeheartedly.

Frank Buchman

Sin brings sorrow, but piety produces pleasure.

J. I. Packer

Command those who are rich in this present world not to be arrogant nor to put their hope in wealth, which is so uncertain, but to put their hope in God, who richly provides us with everything for our enjoyment.

1 Timothy 6:17

"You've *got* to be kidding me!" my wife said.

The famous women's magazine carried a provocative article title as absurd as it was outrageous, something along the lines of "Top pleasure experts share moves so new and naughty, you can only read them here."

My wife turned to me as we waited in the checkout line and

said, "In this day and age, can you imagine somebody doing something in bed and actually thinking, 'No one has ever done this before'?"

I felt chagrined that "pleasure experts" launched such a pursuit, especially since at the time I was writing a book about pleasure—convincing me yet again that God has a great sense of humor and can easily deflate the substantial egos of authors and teachers everywhere.

In one sense, writing a book on giving ourselves permission to enjoy pleasure in the twenty-first century seems like the height of absurdity. Our world *drowns* in pleasure. The economic success of the daily $4 cup of gourmet coffee has spawned any number of "treat" boutiques, from cupcake stores to exotic pastry shops. You can hardly drive a hundred miles on a major interstate highway without coming across an outlet mall or a casino. At home, the Internet offers very specific pleasures designed for very specific subgroups, from card games to shopping sites to podcasts. Every weekend offers sporting events featuring a dizzying array of competition. Amusement parks that operate year-round litter the landscape of most major cities. We have twenty-four-hour satellite television, iPods that can accompany us anywhere, digital movie players that can fit in our back pocket, and enough Harry Potter novels to seriously threaten the world's orbit.

And frankly, the church has gotten a lot of bad press from leaders who haven't handled pleasure responsibly, whether it concerns a sex-related scandal, a lavish and opulent lifestyle, or loud condemnations of gambling or sexual immorality while exhibiting our own very evident lack of self-control with food.

But it is precisely *because* we live surrounded by so many pleasures that we must think seriously about choosing the *best* pleasures. A time of famine makes a cookbook irrelevant, but it can become a bestseller in a season of abundance. Since we live in an age of plentiful enjoyments and pastimes, we need a "spiritual cookbook" to teach us what to do—and what *not* to do—with pleasure.

Wanton Worship

The missionary paused.

She had seen many things in Katmandu, the land of over a million deities, but never anything like this. As Pastor Sam Storms recounts it, "There in the middle of a busy street was a Hindu woman bowing low, chanting and prostrating herself before a pile of yak dung."[1]

Ox manure.

Cow feces.

Bovine poop.

English lacks a nice way to put this. Even so, the woman ignored traffic and the ridicule of others and set up her "shrine" in the middle of the street. She had strewn flowers all over the "pile," decorating her "god" as she bowed in devotion.

Lest we rise up too quickly in judgment, many of us have devotions that are equally absurd. As a college student, I watched in fascination as the god of choice for so many young people—alcohol—put them in similarly absurd situations. They'd drink until they started acting like fools. Then they'd vomit up half a gallon of grotesque bile and wake up ten hours later wearing smelly clothes and sporting a splitting headache.

"And you think this is fun?" I thought.

Once, while vacationing in Hawaii, my family visited a famous destination on Kauai called Secret Beach, formerly a nudist beach. For several years, however, officials had been working to clean it up. Lisa scours guidebooks for "off the beaten path" destinations, and Secret Beach came up as a local favorite. You can't find it easily, but we managed to locate the small road leading to the trail that eventually empties onto a wide expanse of sand.

On our way to the beach, we had to descend a steep trail. My wife sent me down first, to avoid any surprises (i.e., to find out if people were actually wearing clothes) — for taste as much as for morality's sake. I've heard from people more experienced than I am in these matters that a direct correlation exists between those who call themselves "nudists" and those who really shouldn't.

Thankfully, I saw families and couples, all appropriately clothed, and waved my family down. Secret Beach deserves its aesthetic reputation. Without a doubt, it ranks among the most beautiful places any of us had ever seen. About as big as a Texas ranch, the beach seems to go on forever. Way down on one side, we could barely make out some people who might have been trying to keep the historical reputation alive, but we couldn't tell for sure. In such situations, ignorance is bliss. We felt happy with our spot as we laid out our towels and blankets.

Our kids got slammed in the waves as we laughed and played in an area populated by families and honeymooning couples. As I walked out of the water, I looked up to the beach "entrance," a woodsy area that spills out onto the beach, and saw a guy sitting just inside the woods with a telephoto lens trained on the suspect group several hundred yards away.

Here we stood, surrounded by beauty, enjoying family, soaking up the sun — and over yonder sat a solitary young man hoping to capture a few furtive photos to take back to a closed room and further separate himself from the world.

It creeped me out.

In fact, on the creepy scale, it ranked right up there with bowing down in front of yak dung.

I once visited South Africa with my teenage son. On a brilliantly clear morning, the place where we planned to meet with a pastor wasn't scheduled to open for another forty-five minutes. The pastor suggested we walk to a restaurant where we could sit and drink coffee. A casino housed the restaurant — the only place open twenty-four hours — but as long as my son didn't go on the floor of the casino, they would let him in.

We left the brilliant sunlight and the sounds of nature and walked into a pathetically artificial world, with neon monstrosities masquerading as sunshine, and beeping slot machines instead of chirping birds. My son saw a middle-aged man and just stopped in his tracks. The sad fellow looked like an android, robotically pulling the arm of a slot machine as he sat entranced by the glowing screen.

"Whoa," Graham said, and his one-word, involuntary exclamation spoke volumes. Such a beautiful world outside, and this man had left it to become even more robotic than the machine he played. Hard-core gambling at eight in the morning?

As creepy as worshiping yak dung.

We must handle the delicate things of pleasure and desire with due diligence, lest they transform into something monstrous and grotesque. The book of James warns us that unrestrained desire leads to much quarreling and ultimately hatred toward God. We don't get what we want, James says, because we don't ask God for it; and even when we do ask God, we ask "with wrong motives, that you may spend what you get on your pleasures. You adulterous people, don't you know that friendship with the world is hatred toward God? Anyone who chooses to be a friend of the world becomes an enemy of God" (James 4:3–4).

Desire divorced from God becomes decadence. Decadence, in turn, chases away true, godly pleasure. We have an obligation to preserve holy pleasure, in part by approaching God with open, inquiring hands: "May I have this?"

The same earth-based pleasure that feeds our soul with gratitude and leads us to worship and to a fountain of spiritual health may, in another season or in another person's life, become a stumbling block that blinds us to God and the beauty of his kingdom. When I run my pleasures by God—asking him to fulfill me—he acts as my filter, telling me what will build me up and what will destroy me at any given moment. Seeking pleasure apart from God, or outside the will of God, is like giving a toddler a blowtorch to light a birthday cake.

Again, these situations call for sophistication in our reading of Scripture. In the verses quoted above, James tells us that God stands against *polluted* pleasures because they enslave us. But this doesn't mean our heavenly Father opposes the healthy pleasures and joys of this world that come from his hand. If he did, he wouldn't direct us to ask him for what we feel like we need. He's saying, "Let me be your provider. Submit to my providence and trust that I will bring you what will truly satisfy and nourish you."

"Why spend money on what is not bread," Isaiah asks, "and your labor on what does not satisfy? Listen, listen to me, and eat what is good, and your soul will delight in the richest of fare" (Isaiah 55:2).

Here's the great irony: Most people outside the church (and some inside it) think of holiness and pleasure as opposites. They see holiness as the main threat to their pleasure. What a lie! Holiness is pleasure's truest friend.

We find spiritual health in trusting that God knows best, and then in relying on his strength to choose the best. Still, we need even more than discernment to choose the best. Too much of a good thing can sometimes become a negative thing.

Overpleasurers

"She spends three hours a day playing a video game online," the husband complained.

My friend, the couple's counselor, nodded his head and asked the husband, "How much time do you *think* would be appropriate?"

After further discussion, the young couple finally agreed that the wife could play ninety minutes a day. The truce almost shattered, however, when the wife blurted out, "Unless I'm pillaging and looting, of course. That takes at least three hours." (No, I *didn't* make this up!)

Author Douglas Weiss warns about what he calls "overpleasurers." We've been talking mainly about well-intentioned Christians who deny themselves pleasures. Some people, however, make immediate pleasure (however they define it) their highest aim. Weiss writes, "An overpleasurer doesn't live or see life as a balance of relationships, responsibilities, and pleasure. Pleasure moves from a place of moderation to one of prominence. It becomes more important than the duties of family, friends, community, and even work."[2]

One telltale sign of an overpleasurer, according to Weiss, is a sense of entitlement. How do you know if someone sees a particular hobby or pleasure as an entitlement? That's easy. Take it away, or even delay it for a moment. The vicious reaction will give you chills. Weiss writes, "Entitlement seeps in the heart of overpleasurers to the point where if you get between them and the pleasure, you pay. To them, it's as if you were saying no to life itself."[3]

I've seen this in my own heart. Early on in my marriage, I had certain routines, particularly when I took a break for lunch. If my wife interrupted this by failing to get home in time for me to take the car or hand off the kids—thus making me "waste" a half hour or more—I'd act as though she had committed some atrocious crime. I'm not a hot-tempered person and didn't yell at her, but my behavior understandably confused Lisa. Why should such a relatively minor incident trigger such a depth of grievance? Both of us failed to realize my sinful imprisonment by a sense of "pleasure privilege": "I work hard all day. I deserve to get out of the house for lunch when my mind gets tired and I need a break."

To a person imprisoned by entitlement, a "minor" inconvenience does not exist. It becomes a major issue. A golf addict who misses a tee time because his wife got into an automobile accident and needed his help may actually resent his wife for getting into that accident and interrupting his schedule.

As a counselor, Weiss has seen this time and again: "We all know people who, regardless of how sick their child or spouse is, are still going to go do such and such. I enjoy pleasure as much as the next person, but I know that I'm not entitled to it at all times over and above my relationships or responsibilities."[4]

The need to confront this attitude showcases the wisdom of the ancient church. Some traditions of the Christian church — particularly Eastern Orthodoxy — still observe regular days of fasting. In most instances, the fast includes abstaining from meat, chicken, and dairy products on Wednesdays and Fridays. Other traditions choose a favorite pleasure and abstain from it from Monday through Saturday during the season of Lent.

Such acts of abstinence actually preserve the place of pleasure, because they keep us from becoming enslaved by it. If you've developed a sense of entitlement — whether playing golf, eating chocolate, drinking coffee, watching sports, viewing a favorite television show, hanging out with the guys, going shopping, or the like — the occasional fast can bring health and preserve pleasure. At times we must get ruthless in attacking our selfishness and sense of entitlement. I try to remind myself of this, as investing the time and energy required for long-distance running can become a very selfish act for a father and husband.

So while we need to know our pleasures to learn how to marshal their power, in another sense we need to know our pleasures so that we can submit them to the will of God, occasionally sacrifice them on the cross, and refuse to become their prisoner. We must force our pleasures to serve us. As soon as we serve them, what once brought pleasure now brings misery.

The world lives in a cycle of indulgence followed by inevitable regret. Indulgence destroys the soul, and mere regret never leads to change. The wisdom of Scripture and church history teaches us to embrace grateful feasting and seasonal fasting, *both* of which build us up. What makes the difference? Feasting and fasting, unlike indulgence and regret, grow out of acknowledging and worshiping God—feasting in celebration of his goodness, and fasting in recognition of his providence, lordship, and discipline.

The brilliance of Christianity is that it gives us permission to enjoy appropriate pleasure as well as the power to enjoy pleasure without becoming its slave, which in turn *preserves* pleasure for the long haul. What an amazing God we serve, who has set up this world and who eagerly provides abundant enjoyment in a way that blesses his children with health and good things!

Long, Slow Sips

A golf buddy inspired many around him by losing fifty pounds. I felt duly impressed as well. Losing that much weight shows admirable discipline. We stopped at a Starbucks after a round of golf. I ordered my chai tea, and he ordered a venti frappucino, with lots of whipped cream. "I've been good," he said. "One time won't hurt me, right?"

I got a phone call from my wife, excused myself, and stepped outside for three minutes, tops. When I came back, my friend's venti frappucino—which with the whipped cream can easily exceed 600 calories—had nearly vanished.

"What happened to your drink?" I asked. "Did you spill it?"

"No, I drank it."

"Seriously—what happened?"

"I drank it."

"Are you kidding me?"

"It's hot. I was thirsty."

It's one thing to consume 600 calories for a special treat; it's another thing to consume 600 calories and *not even taste them*. My golf buddy lost the weight, but he may not have lost the spiritual weakness that seemed to have accompanied his weight gain.

Another friend, Mark Grambo, makes a helpful distinction. He stresses the need to live *in* the pleasure instead of living *for* the pleasure. When we live *in* the pleasure, we take the time to savor it; that moment becomes sacred. When we live *for* the pleasure, we often get so tied up with expectations, fear, anxiety, and a sense of entitlement that we rush right through it and never really enjoy it. We fear that someone will take it away from us.

A physically fit woman has a daily ritual of treating herself to *one* chocolate cookie every day. She takes a long time to finish her rather small cookie, savoring the flavor and letting it sit on her tongue. In her words, eating that cookie becomes an "experience." Her discipline clearly serves and even enhances her pleasure.

Now, imagine another woman who likes the same cookie—but she doesn't stop at one. She has to eat every one of them in the bag.

Who do you think experiences true pleasure?

Even if the woman who ate the whole bagful has the momentary pleasure of feeling full, eventually her body will have to carry the weight of her fullness, ultimately decreasing her pleasure and adding to her pain. The woman who ate the one cookie will likely enjoy the pleasure of fitness.

Do you see why obedience and surrender to the will of God have such a crucial part in preserving pleasure? Without God's approval, I find no "soul rest" in any action I undertake. Like that woman devouring an entire bagful of cookies, I'll act like a person who has shut down his soul as he rushed forward in a frantic collapse, only to feel overwhelmed afterward with shame and regret. Without soul rest, fear and guilt inevitably follow pleasure.

Heather Earnshaw puts it this way: "When I have even a hint that God does not (for whatever reason) want me to be enjoying something, then I cannot truly enjoy it. Not simply because I must not, but because the ability to enjoy in the abandoned sense ... is lost."[5] The abandoned sense, the savoring sense, the take-your-time-to-live-in-the moment, let-your-heart-be-filled, and rise-up-with-a-satisfied-soul sense—every part of true, lasting pleasure gets erased when sin distracts us with its compulsive and frantic lusts.

We need spiritual strength to truly enjoy pleasure in this world. Without self-control, our passions become perilous minefields of potential spiritual destruction.

Some need permission to embrace pleasure; others need to gain more responsibility and self-control so that they can truly enjoy the pleasures they've previously polluted with a lack of discipline. In other words, as you prepare to take your first sip of a frappucino (or if you are already sucking up the sugary drink with the force of an industrial vacuum), you need to learn how to take long, slow sips, pausing to truly enjoy each one.

How I engage the "little pleasures" often reveals my maturity (or lack thereof) in the grander pleasures of service, intimacy, and relationship. Learning to slow down while drinking a treat can also teach me to slow down and actually listen in a conversation.

Pleasure Serving a Greater End

Dr. James Houston provides a helpful balance to what I've been observing here. He points out that well-being and self-worth come "by looking outwards in relationships: our obligations to others; the duties we perform well; the responsibilities we carry on behalf of others; the emotional involvement we have in the well-being of others."[6]

In other words, seek *first* the kingdom of God and his righteousness, and *then* all other things will be added as well (Matthew 6:33). Do you want a life of pleasure? Order your life on the basis of Matthew 6:33. That's where you'll find true, lasting pleasure.

Dr. Houston points out that when young people don't live this way, they become vulnerable to premarital sex, drug abuse, and other harmful enjoyments. They don't need pleasure, per se — in one sense, they already have plenty of that. What they need is *responsibility*. A young man and woman truly growing in love with each other, actively serving God, building true intimacy, nurturing a sense of mission and calling in life, have much less room in their lives to get inappropriately naked. And they will likely have little or no desire to get drugged out or sloshed.

Redemption involves more than salvation; it includes receiving a new heart with new desires. "Delight yourself in the LORD and he will give you the desires of your heart" (Psalm 37:4). In this context, the wonderful experience of pleasure strengthens us as it renews our souls and supports our calling in Christ. If it depletes us spiritually and undercuts our mission, then by definition it's not true pleasure — not, at least, in any sense that *God* would define true pleasure.

A Long but Glorious Process

Perhaps one reason Christians view pleasure with such great suspicion is that unhealthy souls take pleasure in unhealthy things. As wise King Solomon observed, "A fool finds pleasure in evil conduct" (Proverbs 10:23). Hitler derived pleasure from leading a world into war. An alcoholic derives pleasure from drinking to the point of excess. An abuser derives pleasure from making someone look small or from hurting them physically. Some people derive "pleasure" from sexually reenacting humiliating abuse. Others take "pleasure" from engaging in life-threatening behavior that reveals an inner emptiness, not a God-honoring core.

Pleasure *is not* an absolute good. We can take pleasure in some really nasty things. We can also get into trouble by using *good* things in the *wrong* way. The Latin phrase *corruptio optimi pessima* means "The best, when corrupted, becomes the worst." William Shakespeare put it this way: "Lilies that fester smell far worse than weeds."[7]

When I surrender my pleasure to God's design, my desires become a reflection of his. I find this result to be tremendously fulfilling, though I'm just beginning to taste it. At this point, godly desires have become my refuge, not a threat, and a source of ongoing strength instead of discouragement or temptation. Because we live in a fallen world as fallen people, at times we know that the things we view and desire as pleasure don't align themselves with God; in these instances, it is our adopted-by-Christ privilege to deny these counterfeit pleasures. Renewed understanding will help us do this, particularly when we trust that a relinquishing of the immediate, illicit pleasure means a step toward a more satisfying joy.

When weeks of this God-honoring pleasure pursuit turn into months, and the months turn into years, and the years turn into decades, we will find that our hearts have been turned toward heaven. We will have shaped ourselves to desire exactly the type of pleasure we will enjoy throughout eternity. This comes about not just by accepting the place of pleasure, but by letting God redefine and shape what actually brings us true pleasure.

In short, we must *preserve* pleasure—and holiness is the "salt" that helps this happen.

DISCUSSION AND REFLECTION

1. How has the abundance of available pleasures in the world today actually inhibited our ability to enjoy true, God-honoring pleasure?

2. What makes us susceptible to worshiping "yak dung" (figuratively speaking)? What are some other examples of this that Gary doesn't give?

3. Do "overpleasurers" truly experience pleasure, as God would define it? What are the marks of an overpleasurer?

4. Can you recall an instance in your life when you were surprised at your own vehement reaction when someone denied you a certain pleasure? What did they do? How did you respond? What do you think was the root issue of your response?

5. How might "spiritual fasting" (literally and figuratively) preserve pleasure in our lives? How does unrestricted indulgence ultimately destroy pleasure?

6. Discuss the distinction of living "in" pleasure and "for" pleasure. Can you think of any Scriptures that relate to this idea?

7. Why is it so important to be surrendered to God when we embrace pleasure?

Chapter 10

Dangerous
Pleasures

*I try to diet, but unfortunately I've come to the point in life where
nearly everything disgusts or disappoints me except food. And so I eat
all day long.*

Tony Kornheiser

*[Some prohibitionists] say that wine or such stuff should only be drunk
as a medicine. With this I should venture to disagree with a peculiar
ferocity. The one genuinely dangerous and immoral way of drinking
wine is to drink it as a medicine.... I do not mean that I think the
giving of alcohol to the sick for stimulus is necessarily unjustifiable.
But I do mean that giving it to the healthy for fun is the proper use of
it, and a great deal more consistent with health.*

G. K. Chesterton

*A man cannot be happy in a life of vice so long as he is conscious of
moral scruples; conversely, he cannot be happy in a life of virtue so
long as he compromises with vice.*

A. J. Russell

*Go, eat your food with gladness, and drink your wine with a joyful
heart, for it is now that God favors what you do.*

Ecclesiastes 9:7

It was, and remains, one of the most pleasant afternoons of my life.
My son and I were in Cape Town, South Africa. I had spoken at
the worship services at Stellenbosch Gemeente, a fairly large church

that met in a local school. I have visited each of the fifty states of the United States and many countries, but I have never seen a place like Cape Town. I can't imagine a closer incarnation of the garden of Eden.

Following the second service, a physician came up to the senior pastor and engaged him in vigorous discussion. Naturally, the exchange piqued my curiosity. Perhaps the renowned doctor wanted to contend with some point in the sermon. Maybe a book had solicited a strong surge of opinion, or a political issue inflamed such passion.

On the contrary. The pastor later explained that the good doctor was concerned that the guest speaker might not get served the proper wine for our lunch together.

Now, I wouldn't know a $5 bottle of wine from a $500 bottle of wine. I have no theological issue with alcohol, but as a matter of lifestyle, I just don't often imbibe.

In Cape Town, however, wine makes the world go round. You have pre-dinner wine, during-the-meal wine, and post-meal wine. Every wine has distinct qualities; each one is painstakingly chosen for its appropriateness to the occasion.

The afternoon began with a prayer, commencing our three-hour meal.

That's right. *Three hours.*

We sat outside—in Cape Town, who wouldn't?—looking out onto a vineyard. The relaxed talk, high spirits, and not a single television blaring in the background made me think, "Now, *that* was a Sabbath."

Sadly, however, because of the wine, some believers might call the afternoon a scandal. How, as believers, can we learn to appropriately enjoy the "dangerous" pleasures—the ones that may cause others to fall? Should we even try?

Holding Powerful Pleasures Accountable

The most powerful agents in life must be held accountable. When you go to a Washington state zoo, for example, you see squirrels crawling all over the place and crows perching overhead. Nobody pays attention to these creatures; nobody cares that they run free.

Now, imagine a tiger strolling through the gates or a bear walking near the food stand.

People *would* care.

Dangerous pleasures, in some ways, have much in common with these animals. Sex, a potent force, needs to be contained and held accountable. It carries the potential to do great good — hold a family together, renew bonds of loyalty, create refreshing memories of intimacy, provide relief from the routines of life, create a brand-new life — and the potential to bring great harm. Music can soothe a soul or stir up a riot. An army can protect a nation or attack an innocent one. A fine wine can awaken the taste buds or, in excess, dull the brain and assault the liver.

Because pleasure motivates us, it too possesses tremendous force. Such power must be held accountable, lest it become an evil tyrant.* Money, in the hands of a satisfied, God-honoring soul can do tremendous good. Money in the hands of a spiritually sick person, can become a ferocious force of evil.

A Friend Called Food

When I say "dangerous pleasures," I do not refer only to the ones that come immediately to mind: sex, money, and alcohol. For some people, even the most basic of pleasures, such as eating, can become dangerous.

I once filled up my rental car's gasoline tank at an out-of-the-way

---

* Some astute readers may wonder whether I would include God in this. To them I would say that God's power is held accountable by his own holy nature.

truck stop late one night. The diner remained open despite the midnight hour. I saw a morbidly obese man, barely able to get up on the counter stool, gorging himself on French fries and a bacon cheeseburger. He might have derived some kind of pleasure out of the experience, but that poor man was literally eating himself to death.

What does all of this mean? *To truly enjoy potentially dangerous pleasures without becoming their slave, we need to submit to a God greater than our pleasure.*

When God lets us walk in the land of pleasures, we need to treat these pleasures as though he has given us a power tool or a loaded gun. Certain safety measures can ensure that the pleasure will lead to a happy experience instead of a tragic one. If we ignore God's greater wisdom and his perfect design and plan, we risk becoming enslaved and even destroyed by that which God intended for our benefit. Pleasures have great *power*—God made them that way. We need a corresponding reverence and awe to counterbalance their pull and to direct our hearts to something even stronger.

Columnist Tony Kornheiser talks about the inevitable point in middle age when it seems as though food becomes your truest friend. "I try to diet," he explains, "but unfortunately I've come to the point in life where nearly everything disgusts or disappoints me except food. And so I eat all day long."[1]

No less a light than Augustine* recalled how, after God delivered him as a young man from a daily battle with lust, he struggled even more with gluttony in his older years. A monk can govern his life in such a way as to remove many stimulants to lust, but how, Augustine asked, do you avoid temptations toward gluttony when you must eat to live? Ever-present food always tempts us to misuse it.

I grew up in a conservative Baptist church. Many of the older

---

*Augustine (354–430) was a renowned bishop and author of several classics, including *Confessions*. He may well have been the most influential Christian theologian of the Western church's first fifteen hundred years.

widows wouldn't be caught dead saying "heck" or "gosh," much less their demonic counterparts. They wouldn't think of watching an R-rated movie or, sin of all sins, participating in a poker game. But they would all but clean out the desserts during potluck. Perhaps bereft of many common pleasures, they gorged without restraint when an "acceptable" pleasure sat before them, in much the same way that a climber atop Mount Everest desperately tries to suck down some air.

Kornheiser points out how differently he and his coworker approach food. He writes, "She has had the same rule since she was twenty-five: 'Never eat until you are about to pass out from starvation.' That's different from my rule, which is, 'More cheese.'"[2]

We don't honor God when we become like anorexics, fearing food instead of enjoying it. On the other hand, a lifetime of "more cheese" can literally erase a decade or more from our ability to serve God on this earth. We can eat away our years every bit as much as an alcoholic can drink away hers or a smoker can puff away his. Eating is a great pleasure, but it can also kill us.

We need to be careful when using and abusing the pleasure of eating. What I fear may be happening in today's church is that we have focused on avoiding certain pleasures such as immoral sexuality, materialism, substance abuse, raunchy entertainment, drunkenness, and the like, but we have all but ignored the ancient and biblical warnings against gluttony. We keep pushing the other pleasures away but have made a happy home with daily indulgent eating. When others see the result of our lifestyle choices, they rightly conclude that we may have surrendered our ears, our eyes, our tongues, and our genitals, but perhaps not our stomachs.

It would be a monstrosity of a generalization (as well as a lie) to suggest that being holy means being thin. God creates different body types, and it can be just as much a sin of vanity to spend hours crafting a certain physique as it can be a sin of gluttony to exert no control over our food appetites. So without referring to body size, let me gently ask you this: Does your discipline toward food honor God? Is your witness undercut by your failure to control, or even address, this particular pleasure? Ultimately, only God knows. I raise the issue primarily because it would be simplistic to talk about "dangerous" pleasures and ignore the most common, and therefore perhaps the most dangerous, pleasure of all—gluttony.

Let's now tackle that most contentious of issues: Christians and alcohol.

That Grape Debate

A pastor-friend of mine grew up in a holiness tradition where the only thing worse than going to a PG-13 movie was to be seen in public drinking alcohol. He knows he can't biblically justify an absolute prohibition of alcohol—but in his heart, he also can't accept drinking. He freely admits his hang-up has more to do with his emotions than his intellect, but it is deep-seated and real.

When we began talking about this book, he asked me, "What would you say to me as a pastor if I had a glass of wine at a restaurant and a church member came by and saw me?"

"You're making a big assumption," I said.

"What's that?"

"You're assuming that a church member seeing you drink a glass of wine would be a negative thing. I'm saying it's possible that it might be a *healing* thing for him to see you *responsibly* enjoy life. I'm saying it's just possible that you could preach a very powerful sermon by holding a glass of wine in your hand."

Now, before I lose half of my readers, let me state that I understand the hesitation some Christians have with alcohol. I have no personal agenda to encourage Christians to drink. I never drink beer and drink only a little wine. When my wife and I walked up to a pool bar at a beach in Hawaii and I ordered an alcohol-free smoothie, the bartender responded, "What's the deal? Are you the designated walker?"

I have no history with "hard" alcohol—and absolutely no desire to start one—so I'm on no personal crusade to justify my behavior. If God were to appear before me and say, "Gary, I want you to completely abstain from alcohol," I would find it no harder to comply than if he were to say, "Gary, I don't want you to move to Antarctica."

Let me also say that if my wife had grown up in an alcoholic's home where alcohol abuse had wounded her, as a gift to her, not a single drop of alcohol would ever pass my lips. In some situations I should restrict my pleasure for the sake of others.* A man in my accountability group had a dad with a drinking problem. He says he completely abstains because he knows his family history, and he doesn't trust his ability to handle the power of this pleasure—an excellent reason to avoid alcohol.

And since the abuse of alcohol has devastated so many lives and families, I also understand why some ministries and churches ask their staff members to abstain. These selfless believers willingly forgo a biblically allowed pleasure for the sake of their calling.

Believers have any number of reasons to choose not to drink. But false, self-righteous piety shouldn't be one of them, nor the ambition to demonstrate that I'm "holier" than someone else by avoiding more things than others. And fear that others would think less of me if they saw me drink something that God intended to be received with thanksgiving would usher me into the world of the Pharisees. All of these ugly, sinful, pride-laced reasons to avoid alcohol disgust every bit as much as the practice of getting drunk.

---

*That's the clear teaching of Paul in 1 Corinthians 10:23–24: "'Everything is permissible'—but not everything is beneficial. 'Everything is permissible'—but not everything is constructive. Nobody should seek his own good, but the good of others."

Any reasonable commentator will tell you that when Paul wrote, "Do not let anyone judge you by what you eat or drink" (Colossians 2:16), he intended to defend those who wanted to drink wine or other fermented drink; *no other drinks were in dispute.** Nobody raised a moral issue about $4 cups of coffee in first-century Colosse! Paul tells us, quite directly and forcefully, that pietistic one-upmanship divorced from God's commands—and, more important, his grace—lacks any value in restraining real sensual indulgence.

François Fénelon warns that our spirituality must not undercut our evangelism, particularly as to how we handle "dangerous pleasures." He writes:

> I believe that it is enough to take part in them with moderation, and in the sight of God. More severe, more constrained, less agreeable and disarming manners would only give a false idea of piety to the people of the world, who are already only too prejudiced against it, and who would think that a person can only serve God by a grim and gloomy life.[3]

Let's think about this. The world *already* feels great prejudice against our life and faith; yet certain aspects of belief we dare not render "inoffensive." We need to uphold the message of our sin and God's wrath, and the cross as the exclusive remedy for both, regardless of the unpopularity of such doctrines. But out of compassion for those who don't know the grace of God, who haven't benefited from his forgiveness, empowerment, joy, and life, let's make doubly sure we don't turn people away from the glory of life in Christ by insisting on an empty, fear-laden piety that ultimately has no biblical basis. We worry about alcohol's effect on the church—but

---

*The only possible Old Testament allusions to improper drinking (Nazirite vows—Numbers 6:3; drinks contained in unclean vessels—Leviticus 11:34; and priests ministering in the tabernacle—Leviticus 10:9) are so limited and specific that it's highly unlikely Paul is talking about them to the first-century Colossians.

have we ever thought about our absolutist, prohibitionist effect on nonbelievers?

God did create alcohol, and his inspired Word *does* celebrate it.* Jesus himself made alcohol while he walked this earth (John 2:1 – 11) — and he apparently made some really good stuff. To call alcohol an absolute evil is to ascribe evil to our Messiah and Lord. Do we really want to do that? When Jesus made alcohol, he also made a statement: There is a time and a place to enjoy some good (though potentially dangerous) pleasures.

In reality, moderate drinking *supports health.* A Danish study found that people who don't drink and don't remain physically active had "a 30 percent to 49 percent higher risk of developing heart disease than people who drank, exercised, or did both." As shocking as it may seem to some, "moderate drinking reduced the risk of death among men and women." Researchers found that "among people who were physical [*sic*] active, those who didn't drink had a 30 percent to 31 percent higher risk of fatal heart disease compared with moderate drinkers." The researchers concluded:

> Physical activity and a moderate alcohol intake can lower the risk of fatal heart disease and all-cause mortality. But neither physical activity alone nor alcohol intake can completely reverse the increased risk associated with physical inactivity and alcohol abstention. Thus, both physical activity and alcohol intake are important to lower the risk of fatal heart disease and all-cause mortality.[4]

Dr. David Katz, director of the Prevention Research Center at Yale University School of Medicine, notes that this Danish study

---

*See Genesis 27:28; Numbers 18:12; Deuteronomy 14:23; Judges 9:13; 2 Kings 18:32; Psalm 104:15; Proverbs 3:9 – 10; Ecclesiastes 9:7; Song of Songs 7:9; Isaiah 25:6; Joel 2:24; Zechariah 10:7; John 2:10. Of course, there are just as many verses warning against the *abuse* of wine.

affirms what we already know: "Moderate alcohol intake reduces the risk of heart disease. Moderate physical activity does so, too, and even more powerfully. Combine the two, and the benefits are additive."

Now, "moderate" drinking means one (women) or two (men) drinks a day. When you surpass three or more, you create all sorts of medical problems, including increased risk for heart disease and stroke. In fact, these risks have such severe consequences that medical specialists recommend that "people who can't drink moderately should not drink at all."[5]

These health benefits haven't turned me into a "moderate" drinker. Maybe it's my Baptist background (one I still cherish), but I still prefer to drink very rarely—usually only when social convention dictates it. When God's Word celebrates something, however, and science affirms it, do we act wisely to enforce absolute abstention?

The Bible absolutely forbids many things. It clearly denounces drunkenness, and since God calls us to obey our government (see Romans 13:1–7), all Christians should avoid underage drinking. Prohibiting what the Bible does not prohibit, however, risks pushing people too far, as well as trivializing and lessening the impact and urgency of legitimate demands. Appropriate pleasure gives us greater ability to respond obediently to clear biblical restrictions. Enjoying a good meal, laughter, stimulating conversation, and a glass of good wine, or a dessert capped off with a fine port, not only builds the heart; *it can fortify the soul*.

The church, terrified by the danger, often feels tempted to adopt an enemy/combatant absolutist approach, much like Tony's friend, who eats only when she feels the encroachment of starvation. We sound anti-sex to many because we see the devastation of sexual immorality. Some see us as anti-art because we see the disgusting perversion of pornography. We appear anti-alcohol because we witness lives destroyed by substance abuse. Many consider us anti-music because we question the lyrics of gangsta rap. We appear anti-medication because some people abuse prescription drugs. We sound anti-fun because fun is "of the world."

Such prohibitionist Christians squeeze all the joy out of life—an obscene effect, because when you squeeze the joy out of life, you also end up squeezing part of God out of life. You close yourself off to a glorious, beautiful, and all-inviting side of him. (We also close off many avenues of evangelism, because many of the lost reside in these worlds.)

An absolutist approach to alcohol is cultural, not scriptural. In his book *Radical Reformission*, Mark Driscoll reminds us that John Calvin's annual salary package included 250 gallons of wine for him and his guests. Martin Luther's wife, Catherine, was a skilled brewer, and during a time of separation, Luther's love letters to his wife included several references to how much he missed her beer. And when the Puritans—the *Puritans!*—established their settlement in America, for their first permanent building they chose a brewery.[6]

Once, in a bout of prayer, I made a commitment to be driven by one thing, and one thing only: the reign, rule, and righteousness of God's kingdom—not by book sales, not by reputation, not by invitations or popular acclaim. God made it clear to me that my calling and my purpose must advance his kingdom exclusively. I want God's people to grow in righteousness, and I believe it helps believers to embrace and celebrate true, godly pleasure, lest they become susceptible to soul-destroying substitutes. If wine can lengthen someone's life so they have more years to serve God; if it seasons their soul with laughter and pleasure and so makes them gentler, happier, more contented, and more grateful to God; if it serves as a God-honoring capstone after a day of service and work, then I am going to defend its rightful and godly place in God's church.

I have no personal agenda here, in that I have so little to defend; I don't hold this issue as particularly dear. As a kingdom agenda, however, it is something altogether different.

Addiction Phobia

My daughters have loved dance from their earliest days. Thankfully, a young Christian woman founded a Christian dance studio in our hometown where all forms of dance are taught — lyrical worship, but also modern dance, jazz, hip-hop, ballet, the works. We very much appreciated having our daughters participate in appropriate routines that didn't sexualize preteens and early teens, but during one recital, my wife and I cast an uneasy glance at each other. One dance routine certainly appeared "on the edge" — an admittedly easy thing to do with bodily movement. The girls and their teachers want to come up with something new and creative, and at times they may unwittingly (we believe in the good intentions of their hearts) poke a toe over the edge.

Many pleasures live on this line, which explains why some people object to dance completely. But one routine out of a hundred won't make me yank our daughters out of a school that has provided such a positive physical and even spiritual (they have Bible studies before and after practice) force in their lives.

The same thing could be said of middle-aged guys getting together twice a year to sit around and smoke cigars. I've never smoked a cigar, but when some of my Christian friends do this exclusively on every Fourth of July and New Year's Day, I consider it a bit of a stretch to suggest that their custom seriously endangers their health.

"But tobacco can lead to an addiction," some might say.

Anything can lead to an addiction. Drinking a glass of wine *could* lead to alcoholism. Taking pain medication following surgery *could* lead to substance abuse. Enjoying fine art *could* lead someone to get into pornography. Eating a gourmet meal *could* lead to gluttony. Earning a good income *could* lead to materialism. Playing a round of golf *could* lead to a lifelong obsession. If we never do anything that, in excess, could become a problem, then we need to start sleeping twenty hours a day to avoid all temptation (and even sleeping can become a problem for some — especially those who are depressed).

It comes down to this: The answer to sexual sin isn't no sex, but holy sex. The answer to alcohol abuse isn't necessarily no alcohol (though for a recovering alcoholic, it probably will be), but holy drinking. Here's how G. K. Chesterton argues the point:

> The sound rule in the matter would appear to be like many other sound rules — a paradox. Drink because you are happy, but never because you are miserable. Never drink when you are wretched without it, or you will be like the grey-faced gin-drinker in the slum; but drink when you would be happy without it, and you will be like the laughing peasant of Italy. Never drink because you need it, for this is rational drinking, and the way to death and hell. But drink because you do not need it, for this is irrational drinking, and the ancient health of the world.[7]

Rather than absolutely denying us pleasure, God gives us the ability to enjoy dangerous pleasures within appropriate boundaries. David Powlison provides a helpful list of when such pleasures verge on becoming dangerous threats:

- all that gets obsessive (I'm always thinking about it)
- all that gets impulsive (just do it)
- all that gets compulsive (I can't help doing it)
- all that gets cancerous (expanding out of control, devouring)

- all that gets mutant (unstable, restless, bizarre, inhuman, dehumanizing)[8]

Powlison strikes just the right balance here. Rather than denouncing pleasure in toto, rather than becoming reactionary, we celebrate the responsible use of it. He writes:

> Faced with lewdness, don't become a prude. Faced with luxurious materialism, don't become grimly abstinent and ungrateful. Faced with the unleashing of any and all desires, don't become merely dutiful. Faced with pleasure-loving, don't react with pinched and sour asceticism. Christian faith — the redemption of our humanness — is a radical third way. It is the same alternative both to self-indulgence and to fussy religiosity.[9]

The apostle Paul expressed himself clearly on this use of permissible, dangerous pleasures. While some in Corinth said, "Everything is permissible for me," Paul responded, "But not everything is beneficial," and "I will not be mastered by anything" (1 Corinthians 6:12). I like the New Living Translation's slant on this: "You say, 'I am allowed to do anything' — but not everything is good for you. And even though 'I am allowed to do anything,' I must not become a slave to anything."

If we don't control our pleasures, our pleasures will control us.

One of the most dangerous of pleasures is possessions. That's why I frequently give away or sell off portions of my personal library. I could easily become a hoarder, and these possessions would end up possessing me. For others, it might mean fighting the urge to get a new car every other year, to splurge on yet another new set of clothes, or to remodel the house — *again*. No definitive biblical pronouncement tells us when to replace a car, a wardrobe, or a house's furnishings. The Bible, in fact, often presents such necessities as God's blessing. We can therefore take legitimate pleasure in possessions.

But I find it striking to realize I can't name a *single* thing that Jesus owned, other than his clothing. If you visit the Holy Land, you won't find a house where he lived. You won't find a museum of artifacts — his grooming tools, the art he had on his walls, not even a chair he sat in or a bed he slept in. Yes, he lived in a much different world from the one we live in, but it still hits me that I never see Jesus pictured as buying, collecting, or possessing *anything* — yet he lived with tremendous pleasure and fulfillment. Jesus' story revolves totally around people and never around possessions. We would do well to emulate him.

The Danger of This Book

In some ways, I think of this book as a loaded gun. You can use a gun to defend yourself, help feed your family, or harm yourself. Likewise, the truth contained in this book can help and enlighten, or it can get twisted in many ways:

> "God created food and wine for my enjoyment. If I overindulge a little, what's the harm? I'm not going to let the fundamentalists steal my joy."

> "Sex is good. Pleasure is good. God created both! If I'm not able to enjoy sex in the exact way God commands, what will it hurt if I indulge, just a little, on the side?"

I'm asking you — no, *pleading* with you — to embrace pleasure with sophistication. Pleasure is a gift from God. It is good. He designed us to receive pleasure in many ways and is, in fact, preparing us for an eternity of pleasure. We must also realize, however, that there is a *hierarchy* of pleasure — with God at the top — that orders all of our other pleasures. If the hierarchy gets broken or becomes skewed, then lesser pleasures will begin to war against the primary one, which is delight in Christ.

As Christians, we have an awful tendency to "overcorrect." We see our error ("Oh, so maybe I *can* legitimately accept and even cultivate pleasure. I see how I've endangered myself and dishonored God with a prohibitionist mind-set") and then rush to the other extreme to get away from that error, only to create a new one ("I want to 'eat, drink, and be merry' for the rest of my life!"). Writing or reading a book like this presents exactly that grave danger. Today's church, frankly, has not earned a reputation for intellectual sophistication. Instead of holding things in a healthy balance, we tend to bounce back and forth between dangerous extremes.

Writing a book on pleasure touches both extremes. Powlison warned about this several years ago. He notes how some counselees "exclusively inhabit the obsessive responsibility side, and some live for their pleasures, possessions, and recreations. Either way, they're distracted and driven.... It's a fair bet that at least 99 percent of humankind operate somewhere between mildly dysfunctional and completely crazed on this issue."[10]

Some who read this book, looking for an escape from responsibility, will cling to theological truths about God and pleasure primarily to justify their unbalanced lives of ongoing entertainment. Ruin and misery await them. Others will likely dismiss all this talk about pleasure as superficial, trite permission to live perpetually in a "Disneyland" faith. They risk suffering a breakdown or getting lured into hypocrisy and addiction. Both attitudes—hedonistic license or pharisaic prohibitionism—grieve God.

We find biblical balance in the fourth commandment (the Sabbath). One of my seminary professors, Dr. Klaus Bockmuehl, reminded us that the command to take one day off follows the command to work six days. Some Christians focus on the six days and only grudgingly give in to the day off. Others treat every day like a Sabbath, forgetting to labor diligently for the six days.

When we find the right mix between work and rest/play, we live in the same rhythm as the God who made us. He made us in his image and designed us to operate in his image. Any imbalance—toward either work or play—distorts God's image and design.

For many years, I had an imbalance toward work and responsibility. I viewed the Sabbath as an inconvenient necessity and obligation. If I didn't observe it, I feared breaking down and becoming less effective and productive. I saw it as a tool of the work ethic, a regrettable reality necessitated by the fall, which had left me with an imperfect body and soul. Of course, God observed the Sabbath well before the fall, but we extremists have an amazing ability to refuse to let facts get in the way of our convictions. Powlison's words cut me to the core:

> Here's another curious surprise. Top billing goes to the pleasures of rest, rather than to the achievements of work. The day that is to be set apart for gladness and gratitude is your day off! So restful pleasure isn't merely functional, like a power nap whose only purpose is to recharge your batteries so you can get back to the grind. This rest is not a means to an end; it is the goal itself. Within our daily lives we can get a foretaste of the "sabbath rest of the people of God," when all that needs doing has finally been accomplished, and every wrong has been made right.[11]

I cannot say that I have finally embraced a "Cape Town Christianity," enjoying dangerous pleasures such as fine wine and three-hour meals surrounded by stunning vineyards. When you live in the Pacific Northwest, you can't often sit outside for three hours without getting rained on. But the ability of the South Africans to slow down and embrace even some dangerous pleasures challenges me to this day.

Perhaps it'll challenge you as well.

⟫⟫ DISCUSSION AND REFLECTION ⟪⟪

1. Discuss and debate these questions: If certain pleasures are "dangerous," why even risk engaging in them? Wouldn't it be safer to just avoid them altogether?

2. Gary lists food as one of the dangerous pleasures, yet few people seem to look at the symptoms of gluttony with the same seriousness that they look at other moral failings. Is this appropriate? Why do you think this is so, particularly with respect to today's church?

3. As you were growing up, what were you taught about alcohol? Do you believe Scripture accepts or rejects its use among God's faithful? Given these reflections, what policy would you set for yourself about its use? Would you recommend this for others or just for yourself? Why?

4. David Powlison lists the signs of a pleasure that has become unhealthy: all that gets obsessive, all that gets impulsive, all that gets compulsive, all that gets cancerous, and all that gets mutant (reread the section "Addiction Phobia" if you don't remember what these mean). Given this grid, are there potentially dangerous pleasures in your life that you need to get rid of? Are there pleasures that pass the test that previously you were concerned about but seem with this understanding to be OK? What are you going to do about it?

5. What are some other dangerous pleasures not mentioned in this chapter that can become addictive, and how can Christians respond appropriately? What should guide our decisions in these areas?

6. Gary suggests that today's church isn't particularly sophisticated when it comes to keeping truths in balance, that we tend to embrace one extreme or another. Do you believe this to be so? Why?

7. What is the danger of always siding with the absolute prohibitionists? What is the danger of always siding with the permissive crowd? What is the danger of always living in the middle?

Chapter 11

THE COST
OF PLEASURE

He leads others by the bitterness of privations. As for you, he leads you by the burden of the enjoyment of empty wealth.

François Fénelon

Our present business is to divorce morality from dullness. God never put them together. If in the past, for temporary and specific purposes, man has brought them together, it is now man's duty in the service of eternal ends to keep them apart.

Richard Cabot

Do not be overrighteous,
   neither be overwise—
why destroy yourself?...
The man who fears God will avoid all extremes.

Ecclesiastes 7:16, 18

As a young girl, our older daughter, Allison, fell in love with figure skating. She felt enthralled by the grace and beauty of the skaters' moves, the excitement of the jumps, and even, she once told me, "the sound of the skates on the ice."

At the time, we lived in the Washington, D.C., area without much income. I worked for a Christian ministry that paid Christian ministry wages. Nancy Kerrigan had just won the silver medal at the Olympic Games, and Allison heard that Nancy would soon be visiting the nation's capital as part of a nationally touring ice skating show.

"Do you think we could go?" she asked.

I called the ticket line with great trepidation—and heard my fears confirmed. The tickets didn't come cheap.

"I'll take two," I said with a sigh.

Since I had purchased the tickets so late, I figured we'd sit behind a pole, five feet below the ceiling; but much to my shock, the usher pointed us toward the ice. As we got closer and closer to the rink, my young daughter's face started beaming. She could have lit up the arena with her glow.

"Jesus is really smiling on us tonight, isn't he, Daddy?"

We sat one row away from the ice. I *still* can't figure out how that happened. At one point, Nancy came close enough for Allison to touch her.

Yeah, you need to buy the T-shirt at an event like that. And a couple of snacks. Plus parking. As my daughter and I walked out, I tried not to add up the total cost.

Immediately my Christian mind started thinking, "Wow, that would provide a decent microloan for a poor person in the Third World. You could support another Compassion child for X number of months. With that money ..."

The list ran on and on.

Part of me feels glad that I had some sensitivity to the cost, but part of me wanted to say, "Gary, lighten up! You just created a lifetime memory with your daughter. What's the price tag on that?"

It's a fair question: What is the reasonable price tag on pleasure?

The Latte Factor

Red Cup Day.

If you said this to my kids, each one would immediately know to what it referred. During the second week of November, Starbucks switches from its ubiquitous white cups and ushers in the

Christmas season with festive red cups. Our family is weird enough that we talk about this day before it comes, and then we usually toast it after it arrives.

Just this year, as I poured cinnamon into my chai tea, I got a text message on my cell phone: "The Christmas cups are here!"

I smiled and typed back, "I know; I'm holding one."

Graham replied, "They make me happy."

You can't read my books without coming across Starbucks references. People know this, and once, while traveling, a conscientious couple picked me up. The woman noticed the Starbucks cup in my hand and said, "Have you ever thought of not drinking Starbucks and giving the money to missions?"

I could have responded in a couple of cynical ways. The car they drove exceeded the cost of my Ford Focus by at least $20,000. I could have said, "Have you ever thought of trading in your vehicle for a Ford and giving the money to missions?"

But of course, I didn't. Something about Starbucks brings out the sermonizing in people. I can't count the times I've heard somebody say in front of the church, "For the price of just one latte a day, we could support Hank and Henrietta for X number of months." Financial planners love to use the "latte factor" to show how a daily cup of luxury coffee can decimate retirement planning.

One time, during a small group session, the leader said, "You know, I read that if you buy a latte every day, it will end up costing you $12,000 in ten years' time."

Most everyone said, "Whoa!" but I said, "That sounds like a decent investment."

They thought I was kidding.

I wasn't.

"Listen," I explained, "I've never used tobacco. I can't stand the taste of beer. I don't spend much money on music or expensive food, though I admit I probably spend too much on books. I drive relatively inexpensive vehicles, but I *really* like my daily vacations at Starbucks. I think a decade of looking forward to something and enjoying it on a daily basis is probably worth ten grand."

I'd have a serious problem with myself if we spent more money at Starbucks than we did on giving to missions, God's work, and the poor. I understand why the coffee habit gets attacked. Both materialism and indifference to the poor dishonor God, but beware another danger — making an idol out of poverty, which leads to an ever-escalating and imprisoning piety.

The great Protestant Reformer John Calvin gave this warning:

> If a man begins to doubt whether he may use linen for his sheets, shirts, handkerchiefs, and napkins, he will afterward be uncertain also about hemp.... For he will turn over in his mind whether he can sup without napkins, or go without a handkerchief. If any man should consider daintier food unlawful, in the end he will not be at peace before God, when he eats either black bread or common victuals, while it occurs to him that he could sustain his body on even coarser foods. If he boggles at sweet wine, he will not with clear conscience drink even flat wine, and finally he will not dare touch water if sweeter and cleaner than other water.[1]

In many ways, Calvin showcases an intriguing, somewhat counterintuitive bit of wisdom from the book of Ecclesiastes: "Do not be overrighteous, neither be overwise — why destroy yourself?... The man who fears God will avoid all extremes" (7:16, 18). An extreme fussiness can wear us out.

Particular Piety

While trying to make conversation, I once asked a teenage boy, "If money weren't an issue, what car would you most like to have?"

"A Bugatti Veyron 16.4."

I laughed and said, "That's not a financial issue; that's a moral issue. In a world with hungry people, I don't know how you can justify owning a vehicle that costs more than a million dollars."

But what about $50,000?

To many, that sounds like a luxury vehicle, though in truth $50,000 is about what a standard seven-seat SUV costs when you add taxes and loan costs.

But if $50,000 is too much, then what about $25,000? That's still *more than ten times* what many people make in an entire year in any number of countries, and yet $25,000 will barely get you a new, stripped-down Honda CRV.

How easily we fall into the trap laid out by John Calvin: If $25,000 is too much, then why buy a used vehicle for $10,000? Why not buy a $700 Trek bike instead? Or a cheaper, $250 Wal-Mart bike? And then, of course, you could decide to forgo the expense of a bicycle altogether and hitchhike, trusting God to get someone who paid $50,000 for their vehicle to pick you up and take you where you need to go!

I met an extremely successful entertainer who bought into plane shares so that he could fly on a G-IV worth many millions of dollars. As one who usually flies economy class on commercial airlines up to 100,000 miles per year, I can see why he wouldn't want to be saddled (like I am) every weekend dealing with canceled or delayed flights or sitting next to people who wheeze and sneeze all over you from Chicago to Seattle.

But why should spending hundreds of thousands of dollars seem OK for using a plane but not for a car?

Maybe it shouldn't.

A nationally known pastor whom I greatly respect explained to me why he requires first-class tickets for his travel. He appeared surprised when he heard that I always travel economy (except when

I get free upgrades) and told me a story about the famed Baptist preacher Charles Spurgeon. Apparently, Spurgeon once waited to board a train near the first-class section when a man approached him and said, "Pastor Spurgeon, I see you are traveling in first class today."

"That's correct, sir."

With a smug tone the man replied, "Well, I'm trying to take care of the Lord's resources, and so I am traveling in third class."

"Very well, sir," Spurgeon responded. "You take care of the Lord's resources, and I shall take care of the Lord's servant."

First class or economy; vacation home or rental; luxury car or boat; a daily latte or a country club membership. Countless such issues arise. In a world with so much hunger, for example, do we honor God by spending $25,000 on a party for two hundred friends?

What if that "party" is your daughter's wedding?

Is it poor stewardship to spend $40,000 a year (or more) to send one child to Notre Dame or Wheaton, when you could support the seminary studies of one hundred poor nationals in foreign countries for the same price?

My Christian friend's landscaper questioned him on whether he ought to own a dog when so many people around the world starve to death. "Think about how much you waste on that dog and how that money could feed the poor," he lectured. Of course, it didn't even occur to this landscaper to also ask if my friend should spend money on his landscaping services, trying to keep a lawn green and plants growing in the San Diego heat.

This last scenario shows how blind we can become to certain expenses. Who can easily determine whether spending money caring for an animal carries any more or less worth in God's sight than spending money caring for a yard?

I have all the questions. Unfortunately, I lack all the answers.

But sometimes it helps to live with the questions. In my own case, once I realized that Starbucks had become a daily habit, I gave up two monthly financial obligations, including my membership in the United Airlines Red Carpet Club. I figured I'd rather have a daily latte than a quiet place to sit at airports. As Christians, we need to act responsibly. It makes sense to give up one thing so that we can embrace another. A man might choose to drive a ten-year-old Honda Accord but have a membership at the golf club. A woman might choose to scrimp on furniture but enjoy occasionally buying some expensive clothes. Pleasures can involve great expense, but we can find ways to act responsibly in the midst of them.

Since I travel thirty-five weekends a year, a great afternoon on the road for me means relaxing from a heavy speaking schedule by going for a run and then taking a good novel to the local Starbucks and getting lost in another world for an hour or two. A lot of men get into all kinds of trouble on business trips. For me, having a relatively healthy and, by comparison, relatively inexpensive pastime (one guy confessed that he can drop $200 to $300 nightly at a strip club) helps me live in a way that doesn't undercut my ministry.

Some Christians will immediately say I'm rationalizing. Maybe I am. But I believe I have a responsibility to recognize that God created me with a desire and even a need to enjoy certain pleasures. I want to consciously choose the ones that most serve his cause and the life to which he has called me rather than try to deny a legitimate need and then collapse into an unhealthy, sinful binge.

When my Starbucks routine leads me through healthy pleasures, I'm far less susceptible to unhealthy ones. But all this still raises the question, at what price do life-affirming pleasures begin to cost too much? Always assuming that "cheaper is better" doesn't necessarily square with Scripture, as we'll see in the case of the repentant prostitute.

Let's Be Like the Prostitute

"You *have* to stay at the new Marriott. It just opened up, and it's by far the best place in town."

The man talking to me had talent, fame, a contract with a private jet service—but even more important, he had great hair.

I called the Marriott, and they quoted a price about three times more than what I wanted to pay. A local Howard Johnson had also just opened up and was advertising a Grand Opening special—one night's stay for $59.99.

Sold.

The next day, the celebrity asked me how I liked the hotel. "It's pretty great, isn't it?" he asked.

"Well," I said, shifting my eyes with embarrassment, "I didn't actually stay at the Marriott."

"Why not? The Marriott really is the best place in town. I've been there myself."

Feelings of mortification started dancing inside me.

"The Marriott was a bit out of my price range," I confessed. "I found another hotel that just opened up and had a special introductory rate."

"Huh. What was that?"

Humiliation complete.

"I think it was called Howard Johnson."

I absolutely *knew* it was a Howard Johnson, but in a desperate attempt to reclaim some shred of self-respect, I thought the trite element of uncertainty might win me back a microscopic point of dignity.

A long pause ensued—a gap about as big as the one that separated our stations in life, but only half as large as the one that separated our bank accounts.

Until that moment, I had never met someone who asked,

"Where's the *best* hotel?" I always asked, "Where's an affordable hotel that doesn't advertise that it has color television and doesn't rent rooms by the hour? Oh? It has a paper sleeve around the toilet seat, assuring me that the porcelain bowl has been sanitized for my protection? That's OK—as long as the heating unit doesn't sound like an airplane engine when it kicks on in the middle of the night."

A universe separates those, such as my celebrity acquaintance, who read the menu from the left—to find the dish that sounds most delicious—and those who read it from the right—trying to do damage control on behalf of their bank account before they get to dessert—"If I have the broiled chicken with white rice, my wife can get anything she want. And then maybe we can splurge and have gelato for dessert."

My wife and I grew up, theologically speaking, on Ron Sider's *Rich Christians in an Age of Hunger*, Richard Foster's *Freedom of Simplicity*, John Wesley's pledge to die with less than ten pounds to his name, and the Mennonite Central Committee's famous cookbook, *More with Less*. For years I routinely turned off the shower while I shampooed my hair, as the thought of letting the water run seemed scandalously callous to the greater welfare of the world. To this day, I feel guilty if I keep the water running while I brush my teeth. These things have become ingrained in me, like two lovers' names carved into a tree. I may grow older and more wrinkled, but those names just keep digging deeper into my trunk.

Which explains why Lisa and I rarely took the kids on a truly "big" vacation—an unjustifiable expense, we always thought. We would not be like "those people" who flew out to Hawaii every year or, even worse, bought a second vacation home (while so many can't afford even one).

Now, a quarter century into our family life, while we have a sense of satisfaction that we have tried to give sacrificially, even during some lean years, we also feel an enormous sense of regret.

Last year we splurged on our first really big paid-for family vacation. We became some of "those" people and went to Hawaii. Two weeks, just the five of us. I felt embarrassed when people asked about our upcoming trip, and I'd quickly explain how I cashed in some frequent flyer miles for our plane fare and mention how our family—by the sheer, brutal force of life—was about to break up. Our older daughter already attended college. Our son would be joining her in another year, and our youngest child, Kelsey, not far behind. We wanted two weeks, with no chance of friends showing up, no "just this afternoon" invitations, nothing in my home office to tempt me, so that we could enjoy each other *alone* and *together*.

If that meant putting the Pacific Ocean between us and our neighborhood, so be it.

And I *so* regret we didn't do this every year. We couldn't have afforded Hawaii every year, but I'd tell every family, "Get away at least once a year, just you and the kids." If you have to sacrifice to make it happen, then sacrifice. If you have to beg, beg. If you have to skim off a tiny bit of your tithe, well, that's between you and God, but in some cases, he might well approve.

Just go!

These things entail real cost. But as a young parent, you don't realize that family life is a *season*. Our kids don't stay young, and if we don't take advantage of these moments, we will lose them forever. Yeah, we can "reconnect" in heaven—and let's not discount that—but why not take full advantage of one of life's greatest pleasures here on earth?

In fact, I count this as one of my greatest failings as a father (I can name many, but this one sticks out). Though we did many "fun" things during the kids' younger days (going to parades, fireworks shows, museums, historical sites, etc.), as they entered their teens, I allowed the "family togetherness" to fade as the kids spent prime days with their friends at lake homes or just getting together.

I didn't think enough about regularly planning and injecting family fun times into our weekends and holidays. I felt inclined to say, "Sure," when each child asked about an individual invitation, especially in the face of my own passivity about actively planning something we could do together that everyone would enjoy. (I found it difficult to offer my *nothing* in contrast to their friends' *something*.)

Part of my lack of proactivity involved finances. Part came from exhaustion over trying to make self-employment work as the sole wage earner for our family. Part of it came from not realizing how amazingly quickly kids advance from age ten to age eighteen. Part of it probably came down to laziness.

But I regret all of it.

While crass materialism and irresponsible spending *are* sins, and while God's people *are* called to be generous (even sacrificial) givers, some pleasures—such as "buying" concentrated family time—warrant the cost. We can make frugality a god when we sacrifice family at its altar. In one sense, I had put principles over people, and I doubt my choice pleased God.

If your kids want to go to Disneyland, then save up your money and go. Or make it simpler. Let the little ones see an ocean and pick up a starfish. Let your boy or girl find out what it feels like to fly in an airplane (while you watch wonder overtake over their face).

It's worth the cost.

Remember the repentant prostitute who poured expensive perfume on Jesus, while a few disciples grumbled about the cost, muttering how the money could have helped the poor? Jesus rebuked the *disciples*, not the prostitute. You've probably never heard anything like this in a Christian book before, but here goes: *Let's not be like the disciples; let's be like the prostitute.* Let's occasionally splurge for the sake of powerful and godly affection.

Pleasures come with a cost, but sometimes the benefit warrants the expense.

DISCUSSION AND REFLECTION

1. Name a time when you splurged on a pleasure for yourself or your family. Looking back, do you think this was an appropriate use of money? Why or why not?

2. Do you have any regular small purchases (daily cup of coffee, dinners out, music or book purchases) in your life? Do you think these are appropriate, or do they represent something that needs to be addressed?

3. Gary talks about a woman in a more expensive vehicle than his Ford challenging him on regularly buying a chai tea from Starbucks. How can Christians find an appropriate balance for spending in large amounts and small amounts?

4. Baptist preacher Charles Spurgeon believed it was appropriate for God's servant to travel first class. Do you agree? Why or why not?

5. Read John 12:1–8. What does this passage teach us about expensive luxuries? What lessons can we draw as we consider our own expenses?

Chapter 12

FAMILY PLEASURE

BECOMING A SERVANT OF THEIR JOY

More severe, more constrained, [and] less agreeable ... manners would only give a false idea of piety to the people of the world, who are already only too prejudiced against it, and who would think that a person can only serve God by a grim and gloomy life.

François Fénelon

If we are miserable, it is because we have chosen to say no to joy. The fact remains that God intended joy for us from the start.

J. I. Packer

I have no greater joy than to hear that my children are walking in the truth.

3 John 4

Suffering in the slums of Tegucigalpa, Honduras, had pushed Claudia past the brink of madness. In addition to her mental travails, this young woman also suffered autism. She screamed night and day, expressing her anguish by smearing excrement on the walls.

Jean Vanier, founder of L'Arche, an international network of communities reaching out to people with intellectual disabilities, looks at madness a little differently than most: "Madness has meaning," he insists. "Madness is an immense cry, a sickness. It is a way of escaping when the stress of being in a world of pain is too great. Madness is an escape from anguish."[1]

Vanier points out that many professionals see an extreme case such as Claudia's as a "problem that needs attending." L'Arche workers approached Claudia quite differently: "The Claudias also need laughter and play, they need people who will celebrate life with them and manifest their joy of being with them."[2]

How do you celebrate someone who won't stop screaming? How do you "play" with someone who smears excrement on the wallpaper?

With great patience, heroic long-suffering, and a gentle, super-natural love birthed in grace — that's how. It also helps when you embrace pleasure as a fundamental human need.

L'Arche's methods worked. If you were to visit Claudia today, you'd see a generally peaceful middle-aged woman who occasionally sings songs to herself and who credits *Dios* (God) with making her "happy."

Vanier makes this observation:

> So many people with disabilities are seen by their parents and families only as a tragedy. They are surrounded by sad faces, sometimes full of pity, sometimes tears. But every child, every person, needs to know that they are a source of joy; every child, every person, needs to be celebrated. Only when all of our weaknesses are accepted as part of our humanity can our negative, broken self-images be transformed.[3]

Will we, like Jean Vanier, finally accept our weaknesses as part of our humanity? The sooner we do, the more we'll finally experience and maintain intimacy with each other and learn to fully embrace the conflicted and sometimes complicated pleasures of family life.

Joy in Raising Sinful Kids

I have participated in more small groups than I can count. During the initial "life story" testimony time, each participant, without exception, describes moments of tragedy, weakness, sin, and brokenness, met finally by the strong redeeming grace of Christ. At the end of these exercises, one always senses awe at the pain everyone has felt and oftentimes caused.

And yet parents still manage to seem genuinely surprised when sin and "common weaknesses" manifest themselves in their children. Spouses seem shocked when partners stumble in any number of ways. Though a world population rapidly approaching seven billion people proves that not one of us has ever reached moral perfection — that, in fact, few could even claim to have reached moral *excellence* — we resent each other for falling short of perfection and even begin to define each other by our sin.

This lack of graciousness stops celebration cold. The only chance we have for joy as fallen people living in a fallen world is the gospel of the cross and its corresponding truths of forgiveness and grace. Sadly, however — so very sadly — many Christian homes become places of judgment, accusation, and pronounced disappointment.

Here's the stark reality: If you can't love, celebrate, and enjoy raising a sinful kid, then you can't love, celebrate, and enjoy *any* child. If you can't love and play with a sinful spouse, then you'll never be able to take pleasure in any spouse, for the simple reason that you can't find any sinless kids or spouses.

Let's not allow sin and our universal brokenness to stop our play, cease our celebration, or impair our ability to take pleasure in the company of each other. Parenting books stress the need to raise responsible kids, to teach them discipline, respect, self-denial, faith, and self-control — good things all. But if we sing *only* that song, we'll create tone-deaf, monotone families.

Families begin to break down when they stop enjoying each other; when the husband gives no thought to his wife's pleasure and the wife no thought to her husband's; when parents see kids only as projects to be improved rather than real people to be enjoyed, to laugh with, to play with, to relate to; when kids see their parents primarily as providers and disappointments; when family life offers much criticism but little laughter, plentiful stress but almost no play, a pressure cooker of activities and obligations but no pleasure. Few families will survive, much less thrive, in such an oppressive atmosphere.

If you can learn to celebrate a screaming autistic woman with a disgusting, filthy habit, you can learn to play with your own family — and the results may prove just as stunning. If you wisely put pleasure into play, you can restore broken relationships and maintain healthy, intimate ones.

Transcendent Times

My eighteen-year-old son and I slipped out into the desert air for a late-December run. We had spent a week with my wife's parents in Southern California. On our last full day in Palm Desert, we wanted to take advantage of running under a blue sky, without rain gear, before we returned to the ever-wet Pacific Northwest.

We decided on a nine-mile course, uphill for the first four and a half miles. Running with a high school cross-country athlete is like trying to keep up with a cheetah. Graham's relaxed pace equals my speed workout. A dad can feel old — really, really old — when he runs with his teenage son, but I had reached marathon shape and thought I might as well give it a try.

At the three-mile mark, my son suggested taking a side trail that I never, on my own, would have considered. I obsessively stick to main routes, but I wanted to hang with Graham, so I followed him on the out-of-the-way trail that eventually led to a wide-open desert space, intoxicating in its breadth. We felt like we were running on the tops of clouds.

Grinning now, Graham kept going, skittering up and around a small hill, running like a sure-footed billy goat, while I slowly poked around the edge like a clumsy cow. We eventually reached an even larger expanse and just about fell over at the beauty of the desert. As our heart rates climbed and the sun beat down, we both got lost at the same time in that famous runner's high—something you can never plan or command but feels glorious when it arrives. Even better, after we reached the four-and-a-half-mile point, we turned around and now began running *downhill*. When I checked my watch at the last mile, we had a 6:45-per-mile pace going—which, for me, at the end of a nine-mile run, approaches the miraculous (and for Graham constitutes a barely acceptable "warm down"). What an adrenaline rush!

I worshiped hard and long that morning. I felt so grateful to God, more grateful than I could ever describe, that Graham and I could share that moment together. We've had meaningful talks, difficult talks, and occasionally even embarrassing talks—all the normal father-son stuff that any family experiences—but what a blessing that we could have a time of such exquisite pleasure together.

These are the times I want to hold on to. These are the family moments I cherish.

I remember when our daughter Kelsey became ill with mononucleosis and had to stay home from school. Selfishly, I relished this time, as she and I got to play some games and just hang out (even watching her favorite show, *Gilmore Girls*). Kelsey, ever the last born, acted so perky I couldn't believe it. "Kelsey," I told her one afternoon, "you are the most fun mono patient I've ever seen!"

Kelsey explained that she rested when everyone left so that she'd have the strength to play when someone came home. Sometimes I catch myself getting lost in watching Kelsey talk, play, and laugh. We should have named her "Delightful."

One night I visited our introverted daughter, Allison, who attends Trinity Western University, just across the Canadian border. After we discussed one of her class papers, we walked into a Chapters bookstore. Chapters has "dump sales," where the store gets rid of remaindered hardback novels at ridiculous prices. Canadian stores offer different titles than the ones you normally see in the United States, so Ally and I felt like two kids in a candy store as we picked up books that cost about as much as — or less than — renting a single DVD. Allison laughed at me as I tried to juggle a dozen books. "Your mom will kill me if I come home with all of these," I admitted. "Help me whittle it down to six; that'll just make her shake her head."

Ally smiled some more and cherished the fact that my lack of self-control was making her purchase of just three books look like the height of discretion.

I've described just three vignettes of common family life; I'm sure you have legions of your own. But aren't these times of pleasure the ones we want to hold on to? Families often get obsessed by fear, worry, and concern, primarily about the future and all that could go wrong. Enjoying the present reminds us of all that is right. When we stop building times of pleasure together, we bury the present and its joy under the weight of the future and its threats — like running an engine without oil. The friction will become intense and may well destroy the vehicle.

Let me ask a simple question: Can your children ever relax in your presence? Do they feel as though they receive constant correction, constant teaching, constant rebuke? If so, then why do you wonder that they can't wait to get away with their friends? Who wants to hang around a place perpetually devoid of pleasure?

Some years ago I got to spend some significant time with Dr. Kevin Leman, a renowned Christian author and speaker. Seeing how much his young adult kids relished coming home for a visit compelled me to ask, "How do you build a family like this?"

Dr. Leman gave a simple answer: "If the kids grow up enjoying being together, they'll never want to stop. If every kid goes their own way to have fun — one to ballet, one to soccer, one to scouts, one to baseball, one to youth group — and the family never takes time to play together, once they grow older, getting together will be a twice-yearly obligation, but it'll never be a time of real joy."

Every healthy parenting relationship will require plenty of correction, discipline, confrontation, and instruction. Life is no perpetual playground! But if you build a family in which pleasure gets little or no thought, don't feel surprised if it ultimately collapses into a joyless enterprise — and nobody wants to come home after they finally escape.

Now that two of our kids live away from home eight months out of the year, I want them to remember our family as a place of refuge. I was deeply touched when Allison told me that during the occasional lonely moments of her freshman year in college, she'd go into the bookstore, find one of my books, look at my picture on the back, read a few lines, and walk out. "It always made me feel better," she explained. Home represented a place of connection in a new environment in which she was just starting out socially.

Drink Your Fill

Given the realities of daily life and the grind of making a living and raising a family, a husband and wife who ignore the place of pleasure do so at their peril. If we stop enjoying each other, we set in motion the slow drift that often kills marital affection.

We see one mark of God's genius in his creating the sexual

relationship between a wife and her husband—a completely free act of pleasure, reserved for marriage, that physiologically renews each partner's affection.* All too often, maintaining the sexual relationship becomes just as dutiful as vacuuming the floors—and the marriage suffers accordingly.

Studies have shown that the sexual relationship provides a pretty good barometer of the satisfaction in a marriage. A one-to-one correlation exists between the frequency of sexual experience and the level of contentment within marriage, for both men and women. This doesn't mean having more sex will necessarily repair a difficult marriage. It probably means that when a marriage becomes intimate in all aspects, sex becomes a natural response. The happy husband will want to give pleasure to his wife; the contented wife will want to please her husband.

Some Christian couples need to embrace the sometimes overwhelming pleasure of sexual intimacy rather than feel ashamed or wary of it. It means something, women, that God created an organ in your body—the clitoris—that has just *one* function: sexual pleasure. God designed you to enjoy physical intimacy with your husband. Thinking about this experience, planning for this experience, enjoying this experience, reserving time for this experience, are healthy, holy things to do.

The Bible celebrates giving ourselves over to marital delights. Listen to the masculine voice in Song of Songs:

> How delightful is your love, my sister, my bride!
>> How much more pleasing is your love than wine,
>> and the fragrance of your perfume than any spice!
> Your lips drop sweetness as the honeycomb, my bride;
>> milk and honey are under your tongue.

---

* A man's levels of oxytocin—the brain chemical that leads to bonding and feelings of closeness—are highest immediately following a sexual encounter. In fact, this is the only time that a male's oxytocin levels approach those of his wife.

The fragrance of your garments is like that of Lebanon.
You are a garden locked up, my sister, my bride;
   you are a spring enclosed, a sealed fountain.
Your plants are an orchard of pomegranates
   with choice fruits,
   with henna and nard,
   nard and saffron,
   calamus and cinnamon,
   with every kind of incense tree,
   with myrrh and aloes
   and all the finest spices.

Song of Songs 4:10–14

This man feels *intoxicated* with sexual desire and overcome with pleasurable satisfaction. Far from picturing a weak or shameful act of self-indulgence, the biblical witnesses celebrate the pleasure of the marital bed:

Eat, O friends, and drink;
   drink your fill, O lovers.

Song of Songs 5:1

Reason and Scripture both teach us that God designed us to desire and enjoy sexual intimacy. How generous God is to give us such moments, such intimacy, in a world filled with pain and alienation.

If you've felt suspicious of planning for and deeply relishing marital pleasure, then perhaps you need to take this Scripture to heart: "Eat, O friends, and drink; drink your fill, O lovers."

Serving Your Family's Joy

Serving each other's need for pleasure goes far beyond sexual relations, of course. A wise husband will make sure his wife gets time away from the kids to do something she truly enjoys. A wise wife will encourage her husband to occasionally take half a day to ride his motorcycle or go fishing for trout. Wise parents will make sure they intentionally schedule something fun that the whole family can enjoy—preferably together. Wise college students might even think of planning a fun get-together with their parents to show their appreciation.

Are your children stressed-out with homework and school demands? Instead of asking them if they have done their homework, have you *ever* suggested they take a break and do something fun? David Powlison makes a profound statement: "The men, women, and children you live with need to know ... you are a servant of their joy."[4]

We are to be a servant of our spouse's joy! We are to be a servant of our children's joy! We are to be a servant of our parents' joy! What an incredible blessing; what an honored task. What a pleasure to do this.

Teresa of Avila, the famous sixteenth-century contemplative who founded many houses devoted to prayer, insisted on quiet and contemplation in each house, but she also wisely insisted on two hours of recreation every day—one hour at noon and one in the evening. She explained that these two hours made the other hours possible.

Many Christian families try desperately to do "the right thing" but never pause to marshal the power of pleasure. They deny themselves plenty, but after living without true recreation and enjoyment, they often collapse under the drudgery of daily life.

What does "marshaling the power of pleasure" mean, practically, as it applies to family life? If we see a son or daughter stressed-out over homework, or just feeling down, we can invite him or her to do something that's all about fun. For some kids, it might mean going to a movie; for others, it might mean splurging on tickets for a concert or breaking for a game of Ping-Pong. If your spouse feels stressed-out and you know it, perhaps you can spring for a day at the spa for her.

One husband—a huge sports fan—described to another group of men what his wife had done on the first day of March Madness (the college basketball play-offs). The husband worked an early shift. When he arrived home, his wife greeted him with a plate of his favorite treats. She then led him to his favorite chair, brought him his favorite drink, and said, "You've been working hard; you deserve a day of fun. Here's the remote control, and let me know if you run out of anything."

The other men were all but salivating over that account. That particular day paid huge dividends when she took the time to say, "I want to be a servant of your joy."

One thing that plagues so many wives today is the sense that their marriage has collapsed into utilitarianism: The husbands value them for what they do (earning part of the income, cleaning the house, managing the kids, having sex) and forget who they *are*. They want somebody to love, know, adore, and be interested in them apart from what they *do*. When you take the time to notice your wife's weariness ("Honey, you're overdoing it. Here, let me do the dishes. Go run yourself a bath") or loneliness ("Hey, let's get out of here, have a cup of coffee, and talk. I feel like it's been forever since we've been able to connect"), you affirm that you care. Giving pleasure to your wife (and no, I'm not talking about sex) is one of the most loving things you can do. Your wife won't be one of the many who collapses in tears in front of a therapist in her midforties, feeling taken for granted, abused, and neglected.

As parents, we need to take care, because our desire to raise responsible kids can sometimes crowd out the equally important goal of teaching them how to embrace pleasure. Because we have imperfect kids who often make poor choices, our negative corrections can sometimes drown out positive affirmation. We often say no, but only rarely say yes.

Each of our three children has astonished me with their sense of responsibility. They manage their time far better than I did as a teen. For reasons only God knows, we've never had to push them to do their homework, and we've never had a child waste his or her life with endless video game marathons or obsessive television watching. In this climate, I learned to affirm our son not just when he studied hard or ran a race well or won a scholarship; I affirmed him when he occasionally played Madden football on his Xbox (in high school), and now in college when he takes time out of a packed study schedule to play club ultimate Frisbee. I go out of my way to get excited with our daughters if they invite friends over to watch a movie. I think they should know that I *like* to see them enjoy downtime. For their health, kids need to do something fun now and then. I don't want to be the kind of parent who continually affirms work but only grudgingly accedes to play. Christianity should celebrate celebration. It should foster joy, not kill it.

Of course, if you have an "overpleasurer" child, you'll have to approach this from a different angle. Even in such circumstances, however, don't make the mistake of pitting "all work" against "all play." We need to find a way to help our children *responsibly* embrace pleasure rather than sound as though we oppose pleasure. You'll never find peace if the situation devolves into you being *only* about work and they being *only* about play.

If we are going to be servants of our families' joy—as counterintuitive as this seems to my formerly legalistic mind—we need to be intentional about finding ways to inject pleasure into our homes. Doing this can even become a form of worship, as I discovered when buying a car.

How I Worshiped God by Buying a Car

About 110 days a year, I'm married to a single mom.

Because of my travel schedule, my wife has to carry the load without a husband for almost a third of the year. As our trusted minivan exceeded 130,000 miles, I started to get nervous. If it were to break down while Lisa was visiting our daughter in Canada—and I was away from home—she'd be stranded. I also recognized that Lisa had lost all affection for minivans. The Grand Caravan had served as a wonderful workhorse for nine years, but when we bought it, our tight money situation dictated we get a low-end model—no automatic windows, a lot of little irritations.

Given our family's needs, we couldn't see cutting back on my travel, but I could make sure Lisa had a car that made her feel secure and that she actually enjoyed driving. Once, we rented a car with seat warmers, and I discovered that nothing makes a suburban fortysomething wife happier than warm car seats on a cold winter morning. So when we decided to replace our minivan, a few things became nonnegotiable. We picked out a crossover SUV with automatic windows and *seat warmers*.

As I tried to balance our budget and figure out what we could afford, my inevitable evangelical guilt about spending the money to buy a brand-new car kept pounding at me. We had no plans to buy a Mercedes Benz, but we weren't looking at budget models either. Automobiles have become such a status symbol that I always feel prone to guilt when it comes time to upgrade.

I just don't want to play that game.

As I prayed through all this, I got the distinct sense of hearing God say, "Thank you for taking care of my daughter."

That got my attention, so I listened even more and began to sense God's heart and understand that he, too, felt empathy for Lisa serving as a single mom for significant parts of the year. I believe he felt pleased that I wanted to make her life easier and safer — and even a little more pleasant with the seat warmers. It made sense that he liked the fact that I wanted to look after my wife — his daughter — and bring her joy.

And then it hit me: What, as a father, would I appreciate most — a son-in-law who sat in front of me complimenting and praising me, or a son-in-law who devoted himself to serving and loving my daughter? I didn't even have to think about it. Worship and adoration are essential, but let's keep things in perspective. When I become a servant of my wife's joy, I bring even more joy to her heavenly Father, my spiritual "Father-in-Law."

That's how buying that car turned into a time of worship. Rather than condemn me for getting an upgraded package that included seat warmers, I believe God smiled. When I'm dedicated to loving God's daughter and becoming a servant of her pleasure, God ultimately derives great pleasure from my actions.

On the other end of the spectrum, I've found that about 80 percent of middle-aged men suffer a lot of disappointment with their vocations. Many Christian men often feel trapped by the responsibilities of life — mortgage payments, the weariness of raising kids, the heaviness of staying faithful at a job that may bring little or no fulfillment (and much frustration). Just think how much a wife could serve her heavenly Father by bringing pleasure into such a man's life. Imagine how happy it would make God if she showed empathy for her husband and, instead of hitting him with a to-do list every weekend, surprised him with something she planned that would actually be fun. If you're a wife, you're married to *God's son.* Are you a servant of his joy or a proclaimer of his sin?

Naturally times come when we have to say no to our spouses and children: "No, I can't do that with you, because though it might please you, it would dishonor God." "No, given our current responsibilities and liabilities, that's an irresponsible luxury." "No, that's not a healthy way for you to relax." As backward as this may seem, however, in most instances "No" should be the *beginning* of the conversation, not its end. We need to aggressively and intentionally come up with a corresponding "Yes."

In that light, honoring God's hierarchy of enjoyment and celebration, what can you do today to bring pleasure to your spouse and kids? Has someone wanted something, but, although you've known about it, you've done nothing to make it happen? Have your disappointments stolen the joy you used to feel in seeing your spouse or child laugh and have fun? Will you take a moment right now to ask, "How can I bring so-and-so true, holy pleasure?" Even better, why not ask God, "How can I creatively bring my wife [or husband or son or daughter or parents] *real pleasure?*"

In other words, "How can I be a servant of their joy?"

═══ DISCUSSION AND REFLECTION ═══

1. Is there someone God has called you to serve whom you've stopped taking pleasure in? It's unlikely theirs is as extreme a case as Claudia's, but how do you think your lack of pleasure might be affecting them? Or, if this applies, how do you think your ability to take pleasure in them is ministering to them?

2. How can an increased awareness of our own sin help us to find joy in loving sinful children and sinful spouses? What blinds us to the impact of our own sin?

3. Discuss Gary's statement, "Here's the stark reality: If you can't love, celebrate, and enjoy raising a sinful kid, then you can't love, celebrate, and enjoy *any* child. If you can't love and play with a sinful spouse, then you'll never be able to take pleasure in any spouse, for the simple reason that you can't find any sinless kids or spouses."

4. Gary states that families begin to break down when they stop enjoying each other. Discuss how your enjoyment or lack of enjoyment (with your spouse, children, parents, or siblings) is serving or hindering your relationship with them.

5. Discuss some intentional times of pleasure that you can enjoy with a specific family member in the coming week, either to restore or maintain a relationship.

6. Choose a family member this week for whom you can become a servant of their joy. What can you do for them as an act of ministry?

7. How can we balance our responsibilities to others and our call to serve our families? What's an appropriate balance for spending money on our spouse or children, while also caring for the poor and faithfully supporting Christian outreach?

Chapter 13

Singing
in Exile

Finding Pleasure
in Difficult Circumstances

The most significant thing about any citizen is his artistic attitude toward a holiday and his moral attitude toward a fight — that is, his way of accepting life and his way of accepting death.

G. K. Chesterton

He will never have his full bliss in us until we have our full bliss in him.

Julian of Norwich

When we have found God, there is nothing more to look for in men.

François Fénelon

*How can we sing the songs of the LORD
while in a foreign land?*

Psalm 137:4

Zlata Filipoviæ sounded very much like any eleven-year-old girl when she wrote in her diary about what sounds like an idyllic summer day for a preadolescent: "We gave ourselves a treat today. We picked the cherries off the tree in the yard and ate them all up. We had watched it blossom and its small green fruits slowly turn red, and now here we were eating them. Oh, you're a wonderful cherry tree!"[1]

This pleasurable day, this sweet summer reminiscing, becomes shocking when you realize that Zlata wrote these words in the midst of a war. "I miss fruit a lot," Zlata admits. "In these days of war in Sarajevo, there is no basic food or any of the other things a person needs, and there is no fruit. But now I can say that I ate myself silly on cherries."

Times of deprivation, ill health, and even war don't preclude the need for pleasure; on the contrary, such seasons accentuate the need to find and perhaps rediscover the simplest pleasures of all.

Jesus modeled how to embrace the simplest of pleasures in what could have been an oppressive atmosphere. He certainly never lived in opulence; he didn't even own a home. Though we never hear about him getting sick, he was persecuted, lied about, misunderstood, and attacked. In the midst of this hardship, Jesus didn't just grit his teeth and press on; nor did he hide away in endless solitude to wallow in self-absorbed misery. On the contrary, have you ever noticed how frequently we see Jesus engaged in perhaps the most fundamental pleasure of all—earnest conversation? He talks to religious people, poor people, and sinful people. He talks to his disciples and his followers. A constant stream of dialogue seasoned Jesus' life.

Living in a day in which pleasures came rarely (the Jews suffered under Roman occupation *and* Pharisaic extremism), Jesus modeled how to embrace the most basic (and inexpensive) of pleasures in the midst of destitution—the entirely free and rewarding art of relationship.

We, too, must find our own "pockets of pleasure" in the midst of difficult and trying circumstances.

Holy Discontent

Perhaps you have wondered how this concept of marshaling the power of pleasure can exist outside the comforts and affluence of the West. Or maybe you question how it applies in lives with more than their fair share of misery.

What do we say, for instance, to a woman married to a man who just isn't as "into" God as she is? She'd prefer to live in service to her heavenly King; her husband would prefer to go to church once a month, provided it's not hunting season, the Chicago Bears aren't playing, or he didn't get into bed after 11:00 p.m. on Saturday night.

In such a life of marital deprivation, a time will come when the wife has to admit that the pleasure she longs for may never happen — and then organize her life accordingly by developing other meaningful friendships in which she can share her faith. Doing so doesn't dishonor God's ability to transform a person's heart in the future, but it does guide the wife to seek God's alternate provision in the midst of her current disappointment.

How does a parent find pleasure when a beloved child fights what doctors call an "incurable" disease — and God doesn't seem inclined to heal this child? How does a man find pleasure in unemployment while daily struggling against rejection, humiliation, financial pressure, and stress? How does someone who uses a wheelchair deal with never-ending limitations? When people disappoint you, hurt you, and let you down, how can you draw from the wells of God's love, spiritual nurture, emotional provision, relational care — and even pleasure?

We must address these situations head-on, because if what I've said is true — namely, that neglecting holy pleasure makes us vulnerable to illicit pleasure — then just when we need God the most, our inability to marshal the power of pleasure may tempt us to abandon all that we know as good and right.

Earlier I pleaded for us to become more sophisticated in our thinking. We need this wisdom especially here. Spiritually speaking, we need to embrace and appreciate the place of pleasure for spiritual formation; but in some lives, and in some seasons of life, certain pleasures will become unavailable to us or so colored by our disappointment and sorrow that even the most delectable of life fruits seem bitter to our souls. In these instances, Jesus cuts right to the heart of the matter and points us back to him. Let's see how he did this in one of his most famous encounters.

The Anti Dr. Fix-It

She may be the most famous multiple divorcée ever known. After racking up five husbands and at least one lover, she appeared to feel comfortable around men. But she had never met a man like *this*.*

His first request sounded simple: "Please give me some water. I'm thirsty."

Have you ever lived as a true outsider? If you haven't, you can't possibly imagine what it feels like for someone to say, "You belong." That's what Jesus communicated to the Samaritan woman in the mere act of talking to her. The geographical dispute about the proper place for the holy temple had created centuries of acrimony between Jews and Samaritans. The historical DNA of her ancestors had kept her anathema to any respectable Jewish man, and even more to a prophet. She had no way to get away from this ostracism, for all that caused it coursed through her blood—a Samaritan, an outcast, wanted by many Samaritan men but never by a *real* Jew.

Yet here came a Jewish man, a rabbi and a prophet no less, asking *her*, a Samaritan woman, for a drink.

When the woman points out the absurdity of the moment, Jesus reveals something to her that he had spoken of only indirectly to the "real" Jews. Jesus announces, point-blank, that he is the Messiah.

What an extraordinary pronouncement! God's chosen people,

---

* This story is told in John 4.

presumably the ones who had the temple in the "right" place, had to glean the truth about Jesus' messiahship through parables, indirect allusions, and scriptural applications. But not this woman! She gets the truth in its most naked form. Even a simpleton couldn't have missed Jesus' meaning: "I who speak to you am he" (John 4:26).

Ultimately, she needed to hear nothing else.

Notice that throughout this famous conversation, not once does Jesus talk to the woman about how to "fix" her relationships with men or find "true pleasure" in human intimacy. This never becomes a "Dr. Fix-It" moment, because Jesus cuts to the core of her deepest need—she needs to stop looking at men to find fulfillment and turn to God. Because of the way she has lived, she will never know the intimacy of a lifelong marriage as God intended. Her actions have blown apart that possibility. But Jesus speaks of something even deeper and richer than a rewarding marriage—a relationship with God himself. This is the pleasure she must seek. A "happily" married woman, absent the Samaritan woman's desperation, might miss such devotion. The Samaritan woman's sin ironically becomes her servant when it points her back to God, and God alone.

At a certain point, we may have to realize we're not going to get what we think we need. I receive emails all the time from people who have made a mess of their lives. The battles between their current spouse and their children from a previous spouse create daily trials. The hurt they've caused and felt because of unfaithfulness, drug or alcohol abuse, financial mismanagement, or the complexity they've brought into their lives by disobedience keeps them weighed down. "The best," as they formerly defined it, is no longer an option and never will be.

While pleasure has a place, it serves a prior passion. Jesus points this woman to that passion. He speaks to her about worship, about a drink that will completely eradicate her thirst: "Ask *me* for a drink, not the five previous husbands who didn't work out or your current live-in lover. If you truly realized who you're talking to, you'd find your satisfaction in me." If Jesus had simply told her how to "fix" her relationships with men, he would only have given her emotional water that eventually would leave her thirsty. "Anyone who drinks this water will soon become thirsty again." The water Jesus offered truly quenches: "But those who drink the water I give will never be thirsty again. It becomes a fresh, bubbling spring within them, giving them eternal life" (John 4:13–14 NLT).

That's What You Asked For

Talk to an addict of any stripe (food, substance abuse, etc.), and they'll often blame a parent, a spouse, cruel bullies, an authoritarian teacher, or an unfair government that "forced" them into self-medicating their pain. Behind these defenses you find the seriously flawed thinking that such disappointments and betrayal are uncommon and unique.

In fact, the Bible all but promises us that those we love the most *will* betray us. We should *expect* betrayal. Jesus warns us, "You will be betrayed even by parents, brothers, relatives and friends, and they will put some of you to death. All men will hate you because of me" (Luke 21:16–17). David spoke of a vicious betrayal: "Even my close friend, whom I trusted, he who shared my bread, has lifted up his heel against me" (Psalm 41:9).

If a close friend or family member hasn't betrayed you, *you're unusual*. Since I travel to so many churches, I often communicate this message to frustrated and hurt pastors. Some of them struggle to understand how a friend could have betrayed them. Maybe they thought a staff pastor or an elder or deacon "had their back" but then stabbed them in it. In fact, very few pastors have escaped betrayal by a close friend. Acting as though yours is an unusual situation will never help. *To be called into ministry is to be called into a world in which you will be persecuted and betrayed.*

Supreme Court Justice Clarence Thomas has a refreshing perspective, gleaned from his experience of running the Marine Corps Marathon in his early thirties:

> Midway through the race, I ... hit the "wall" I'd heard so much about from my fellow runners. My legs grew stiff and I felt as though I was on the verge of collapsing. *Never quit, never quit,* I whispered over and over again, the same way I had throughout my training, but it didn't help this time. My body begged me to give up with every tortured step, and I barely made it to the next water stop, which was in the parking lot of the Pentagon. A young black Marine was handing out water to the exhausted runners. "... This is hard," I told him. "That's what you asked for," he replied without a trace of sympathy. I shook off my self-pity, picked up my pace, and crossed the finish line three hours and eleven minutes after I'd started.[2]

That's what you asked for.

You have several kids, one of whom is making some really bad choices. Do you think you can raise human beings who "stumble in many ways" (James 3:2) and *not* bear the pain of their rebellion?

That's what you asked for.

You married a sinner who stumbles in many ways, or you live in a dorm or hall surrounded by people who don't know God, and you feel *surprised* that these relationships can hurt and frustrate you?

That's what you asked for.

You live in an imperfect body, and you're surprised that it's now sick or injured or in pain?

I don't mean to sound harsh, but honestly, we are very vulnerable in this world. Pain and suffering — whether emotional, physical, or spiritual — are not only common but *universal.*

In this world, we must learn how to draw from this well of life when our own well seems dry and empty and pleasures seem particularly hard to come by.

What Not to Do

Before we explore what we should do, let's list some things we shouldn't do when our well seems dry—things that only take us further away from life and true pleasure.

We Shouldn't Become Distracted by Sin

When you feel "dry," that's the time to especially beware of the false allure of seemingly pleasurable sin. Though it may not *feel* like a step in the wrong direction, it always is. In his book *Future Grace*, John Piper wisely points out, "The power of sin is the false promise that it will bring more happiness than holiness will bring. Nobody sins out of duty. Therefore, what breaks the power of sin is faith in the true promise that the pleasures of sin are passing and poisonous, but at God's right hand are pleasures forevermore."[3]

Insist on true, holy pleasure—or *nothing at all*.* I plead with married people to see sexual temptation of any form as a call for them to become more intimate with their spouse. Intimate doesn't necessarily mean "sexual." It means that God created hormones, and when we notice that they are particularly alive and active, it's God's way of telling us we need to tend to our marriage (on all levels). This commitment to pay renewed attention to our spouse is the only holy response to sexual temptation: "Oh, I see I'm sexually tempted; how am I doing with my mate?" What Satan intends for harm, God can use for good, for building up our home instead of

---

* The "nothing at all" phrase comes from the ancient Christian virtue of detachment, which gets far too little attention today. My book *The Glorious Pursuit* (Colorado Springs: NavPress, 1998) devotes a chapter to this virtue.

tearing it down. You will literally change your life and your marriage if you begin using sexual temptation as a call to evaluate and improve your relationship with your spouse. *Turn the temptation into spiritual reflection and personal evaluation* (but be aware that the temptation could signal a growing coldness toward God as well, not just toward your spouse).

If you're single, you can use sexual temptation as motivation to build a healthy and holy relationship that may lead to marriage. Running off to a computer screen or arranging a quick "hookup" isn't going to help you find someone worthy of marriage; these activities only make you *less fit* for marriage. Don't do anything that would interfere with your future marriage. Insist on building healthy, productive, God-honoring relationships.

If your loneliness causes you to run to the casino or gorge on a bag of potato chips, your choices are fighting against your ultimate pleasure. You'll be less attractive as a marriage partner due to financial problems or a lack of physical fitness, and your loneliness will only increase.

When we feel vulnerable, we need to strictly evaluate our pleasures, running them through a fine filter, making sure they're free of pollutants before we breathe them in. Immediately turning to sin to deal with disappointment, deprivation, or hurt is like smoking cigarettes to lose weight. In the short term, it may seem to help; in the long term, it creates an even bigger problem.

We Shouldn't Stop Serving

The older I get, the more I value ministry. Though I understand the notion of "*being* over *doing*," I think pitting the two against each other can be misleading. In a healthy life, the two build on each other rather than compete. My days get their meaning from honoring and glorifying God — that *is* my being. In the words of

Jesus, "I have brought you glory on earth by completing the work you gave me to do" (John 17:4).

Our spiritual enemy wants to use our disappointments to get us turned on ourselves so we become self-focused, self-commiserating, self-centered. Yet Jesus tells us that ministry energizes us (and ultimately gives us pleasure) more than anything else. He said to his disciples, "I have a kind of food you know nothing about.... My nourishment comes from doing the will of God, who sent me, and from finishing his work" (John 4:32, 34 NLT).

Sin scars all human relationships, as rewarding as they can be; thus, on their own, they will never permanently fulfill us. We draw spiritual energy and life from obeying the God who made us and allowing him to use us in whatever sphere of life we find ourselves.

In many ways, mission provides one of the highest pleasures of life. Watching God's kingdom advance and knowing that God has used *you* to gain this sacred piece of ground gives a pleasure that few things can match. Over time, we become excited seeing God move, even when we had nothing to do with it. I once read two books back-to-back—one by Tricia Rhodes (*Sacred Chaos*) and one by Kay Warren (*Dangerous Surrender*).[4] Both books detail marvelous testimonies of God's work through godly women living in the glorious prayer, "Your kingdom come, your will be done on earth as it is heaven."

My heart felt nearly overwhelmed as I prayed, "Thank you, Lord, for moving so many people to care so deeply. You take us as selfish consumers, and you turn your children into compassionate people who care."

I sat in prayer, soaking up the pleasure of meditating on God's way with his people. I took pleasure in the fact that God reveals himself to the world in the way he transforms us into his image. I took pleasure in the reality of God chasing away some of the loneliness and ugliness of this present world with the beauty of love and selfless service. I took pleasure in the hope that God remains always on the move. Yes, people still get cancer, lose their jobs, or watch loved ones die—soul-shaking realities in a fallen world. But God is on the move, *always*! Teens, who only months before were blinded by their narcissism, take up the cross and become active agents of change. Married couples on the brink of divorce learn how to love and become walking testimonies of God's power to reconcile hearts. Addicts who lived for years with the bitter taste of defeat and despair now walk in joyous victory and happy hope. Oh, how beautiful, how wonderful, how glorious when we see God on the move!

Take this universal truth—God is on the move—and draw hope and purpose from it to attack the natural self-focus that arises from painful personal trials. If your child lies in the hospital, keep praying for the nurses and doctors who visit your room. If you've lost your job (or are still seeking your first one), ask God how he can use the new contacts you're forced to make to reach out to others.

Even if you're sick or in pain; unemployed; divorced, widowed, or frustrated in your singleness; addicted or worn-out—if you know God, those who don't know him still have a greater need than you do. Reach out to them. Embrace the pleasure of seeing God's kingdom spread, even in desperate situations. It will feed you in a way that nothing else can and will bring an even deeper dimension of pleasure into your life—one you might have missed had you never walked through this dry season.

We Shouldn't Feel Sorry for Ourselves

Since every one of us lives and relates to people who "stumble in many ways" (James 3:2), we all have legitimate complaints. Maybe it's your parents; maybe it's your kids; maybe it's your spouse. Feeling sorry for yourself won't solve anything. It just uses up energy best used in addressing the problem.

I've met husbands who care for wives suffering from Alzheimers, wives who are married to husbands with health issues that make full expressions of physical intimacy all but impossible, and kids who ache because their parents will never get emotionally or spiritually healthy enough for them to have a meaningful relationship. Only when they stop focusing on what they've lost and instead become grateful for what they do have, or what they might work toward, do they find true joy and lasting pleasure.

Recently I talked to a godly young man named Brian who suffered severe burns in an industrial accident more than a decade ago. He lost 90 percent of the skin on his body, lost his eyesight, and had two arms and one leg amputated. As we spoke, I felt astonished by his utter lack of self-pity; on the contrary, he expressed great thanks for how God used the injury to cement his faith. He has become a tower of strength, and as he described his relationship with his wife, I was struck by the obvious intimacy of their relationship on all levels, even in the face of such a debilitating injury. In fact, Brian even told me, "I've had less bad days after the accident than before."

I compared his Christlike spirit with my own whining when I suffered a running injury and had to take a few weeks off—and I just sighed. In a fallen world we can develop a radically unrealistic perspective. One severely disabled man said, "When you're a quadriplegic, you look at a paraplegic and think, 'Man, they've got it made!'"

When we feel sorry for ourselves, we work against finding positive solutions. Self-pity destroys the can-do attitude that learns to feed off of available pleasure. Brian can't see his wife, and he'll never be able to hug her, but he can talk to her, pray with her and for her, and comfort her with his wise words of love, care, and concern. Through the Internet, he has even recently discovered ways to buy her presents without her knowing about it ahead of time.

Sometimes, in God's providence, certain pleasures may be closed to us. God says, in effect, "This is not for you, at least not now." We have to trust him to provide alternate pleasures—perhaps of an entirely different sort—that will sustain us in our trials.

Feelings of entitlement feed anger; feelings of thankfulness swell our souls and can make us tear up with overflowing gratitude. Thanking God helps us recognize what pleasures we do have while at the same time *increasing* our pleasure.

Pleasure Prescriptions

To remain faith-filled and to retain our joy in unpleasant situations, we should strive to find pleasure where we can. I talk to women all the time whose husbands have abandoned them. They want to know what they should do while they work and pray for reconciliation.

They frequently express shock when I stress the importance of learning how to enjoy life as a single mom. "Find new pleasures," I tell them. "Rediscover laughter. Work on appropriate same-sex relationships. The best way to attract a man isn't by nagging him to return or trying to use your children to make him feel guilty; it's by building a life that he wants to rejoin."

If your children are rebelling, if you're losing your job, if your church is crumbling, if your health is failing—whatever the situation—find *some* pleasure to cultivate. Work hard to draw from an appropriate well. Some waters will be closed to you, but God never fails to open up others. You may find that worship practices once considered routine will take on a new dimension, an increased richness, as you savor your walk with God. You may even begin to discover the pleasure found "in weaknesses, in insults, in hardships, in persecutions, in difficulties" for Christ's sake (2 Corinthians 12:10).

An article in *USA Today* highlighted the struggles of people suffering from chronic illness or other long-term stresses. Here's what some of them found to be spiritually therapeutic. Notice the wide variety of responses:

- A woman with severe scoliosis, severe arthritis, and chronic "mind-numbing" pain: "I take about an hour each afternoon to brew myself a cup of Irish tea with cream and sugar.... Some days I can hardly wait for my afternoon ritual, as it restores my soul."

- A middle-aged woman born with a heart defect who has had lifelong heart problems: "The things I do when I need to lift my spirits are to read a book (historical romance), take a bubble bath with candles burning, and just spend time with my [family]."

- A man struggling with prostate cancer and depression: "I found that getting out of the house and talking with anyone can snap me back to better spirits."

- A woman with multiple stress points: "No matter the season or weather, I walk my horse out to the field and watch him contentedly graze."

- A woman who experienced two recent family deaths and has a son stationed in a combat zone listens to Celtic and old country music, laughs at *America's Funniest Home Videos*, and invites a cat or two to share her recliner. She says, "Stroking their fur and listening to them purr always lifts my spirits."[5]

As you walk your own difficult road, keep in mind that even heroes need to eat. Even heroes need to laugh. Even heroes eventually need to rest. If God has called you to heroic faith, do what you must to build yourself up so that God can keep pouring you out.

Finding Our Heaven in Jesus

In the fourteenth century, as the Black Death decimated Europe's population, Julian of Norwich thought she was lying on her deathbed. In this time of little hope and much fear, this remarkable woman wrote, "It has always been a comfort to me that I chose Jesus for my heaven, through his grace, in all this time of suffering and sorrow. And that has been a lesson to me, that I should do so for evermore, choosing Jesus alone for my heaven in good and bad times."[6]

Don't you just love that phrase? *Jesus is our heaven*. Regardless of what's happening to us or in the world around us, if Jesus is our heaven, then our heaven and our pleasure remain secure in him. Julian courageously found this comfort even in the midst of a ghastly plague.

C. S. Lewis has famously helped us see that part of pleasure's purpose is to reveal that even the most intense pleasure on earth won't last—and that this gives evidence of eternal pleasures waiting for us to which this world can point but never match.[7]

When our greatest delight is knowing Christ—and God made us to have no greater delight—the queen of pleasures, the pleasure of all pleasures, always *remains with us*, regardless of our circumstances. Jacques Ellul put it so eloquently: "The hope of Jesus Christ is never a dash of pepper or a spoonful of mustard. It is bread and wine, the essential and basic food itself."[8]

As a young college student, I was blown away by Paul's unadulterated passion for Jesus, expressed in his letter to the Philippians. He writes as a servant of *Christ Jesus* (1:1), to the saints in *Christ Jesus* (1:1), offering grace and peace from the *Lord Jesus Christ* (1:2).

Two verses—and he mentions Jesus three times.

Paul encourages the Philippians with assurances of the day of *Christ Jesus* (1:6), mentioning how much he loves them with the affection of *Christ Jesus* (1:8) and reveling in the fact that they might be filled with the righteousness that comes through *Jesus Christ* (1:11). He reports that he is in chains for *Christ* (1:13) but takes confidence in the help given him by the Spirit of *Jesus Christ* (1:19). His greatest prayer, "now as always," is that *Christ* will be exalted in his body (1:20); for to Paul, "to live is *Christ* and to die is gain" (1:21, emphasis added).

To those outside the faith, death ends all pleasure and stops all delight. Yet Paul preferred death to this life, because death provided the doorway for him to behold his ultimate pleasure, Jesus, face-to-face.

If I have trained myself to find my pleasure in God; if I receive each sunset as a mark of his handiwork; if I consider the beauty of my wife's form as the image of his loveliness, or the laughter of a small baby as the sound of his joy, or the majesty of a mountain as the mark of his greatness, or the brilliance of a song as the sound of his harmony—then I will feel overwhelmed at death, as all these pleasures will finally, amazingly, overwhelmingly, come together in one place, in one person, at one time.

During a run, as Keith Green's "Oh Lord, You're Beautiful" poured through my iPod, it dawned on me that, in one sense, there can never be a full hell for me. I hope this isn't heretical, but even if I were in hell, the thought that God was finally getting his due, that everyone knew he was God, that he had reconciled the world to himself and was being worshiped, that he had fully defeated the powers of sin and death, and that everything was now in submission to him—all that would cause such joy that it is difficult for me to imagine being miserable. Now, undoubtedly, this disposition is a mark of God's redeeming grace (I'm *not* suggesting it is universal), but the future anticipation of God being universally worshiped and acknowledged as the reigning King gave me such a vision of future joy that I could scarcely contain myself in the midst of such bountiful pleasure.

If I find my pleasure in Starbucks alone, I am at the mercy of a company that may go out of business. If I seek my pleasure in sex alone, I make myself vulnerable to a fading, aging body — as well as to the cooperation of a partner. If my pleasure is in a business, I remain subject to the whims of my consumers. But if my life has been a single journey always pointing me to find my fulfillment in God — urging me to see each earthly pleasure as a reflection of his kindness, goodness, and love — then my ultimate pleasure has become more certain than anything this world can offer.

Even in the most difficult of circumstances.

DISCUSSION AND REFLECTION

1. As you look back on your life, what has been one of the most difficult seasons you've ever faced? Did you find any simple pleasure that helped you persevere? If so, what was it?

2. How would you counsel someone in difficult circumstances —a serious illness, divorce proceedings, unemployment, child rebellion—to intentionally cultivate little pleasures where they can?

3. Gary lists several warnings for those facing difficult circumstances: beware the distraction of sin, don't stop serving, and don't feel sorry for yourself. Discuss why these become particularly acute temptations when we are disappointed or discouraged.

4. How can Christians discover practical ways to "find their heaven in Jesus" when everything else seems like such a disappointment?

Chapter 14

HILARIOUSLY HOLY

A happy heart makes the face cheerful,
but heartache crushes the spirit....
All the days of the oppressed are wretched,
but the cheerful heart has a continual feast.

Proverbs 15:13, 15

I should regard any civilization which was without a universal habit
of uproarious dancing as being, from the full human point of view, a
defective civilization. And I should regard any mind which had not
got the habit in one form or another of uproarious thinking as being,
from the full human point of view, a defective mind.... Unless a man
is in part a humorist, he is only in part a man.

G. K. Chesterton

If we can't open the pressure valve with laughter, we just might ex-
plode. So laugh or die. It's up to you.

Kevin Harney

Humor is redemptive when it leads to comic self-discovery.

Elton Trueblood

While serving on a pastoral search committee, I listened to hours of
sermons from people all over the country. One earnest young appli-
cant clearly aimed for conviction. His résumé hit our benchmarks,
so I eagerly listened to his talk. The first sermon seemed really
heavy, but he delivered it on a Good Friday after all, so I expected

no less. When I listened to another one, however, he evoked the same heaviness. I listened to a third and even the start of a fourth, wanting to embrace his ministry for our congregation.

But I just couldn't.

As the committee discussed his sermons, we came to a general agreement that he didn't provide a good fit for our congregation. I finally put our uncertainty into words: "I wonder if he has any joy in life. Where is the joy of life in Christ, the satisfaction of living in worship of and relationship with God?"

He preached well with regard to conviction, reminding us of responsibility and duty and obligation—but on the scale of modeling an inviting life, he ranked no higher than a two or three out of ten.

Why would somebody want to follow such a somber, almost dreary persona?

Even Teresa of Avila, who became feared, controversial, and indeed *hated* in her day for attempting to bring discipline and asceticism to a lax convent of Carmelite nuns, once said, "From silly devotions and sour-faced saints, good Lord deliver us."[1] She believed in self-discipline and self-denial—but self-discipline and self-denial without joy and pleasure soon become warped walls. Over time, the rain will seep through the cracks and eventually compromise the entire structure. Teresa taught her followers that embracing God's simple pleasures prepares us to endure ascetic self-denial.

Do not forget this: discipline without joy eventually leads to cruelty, arrogance, and condemnation. It is not an avenue of life, but rather a dead end of desperate performance. Instead of inviting people to embrace and engage in life, it attempts to pull self-hating people back into misery, and sometimes even causes them to *glory* in that misery.

Perhaps this was part of the reason Jesus told his disciples not to look "somber" (NIV) or "dismal" (RSV) when they fasted (Matthew 6:16). Certainly, the primary point of this passage is to warn against fasting for show—and an overly somber look would do just that. But I also wonder if Jesus doesn't see himself and others turned off by followers who confuse grimness with godliness. In one sense, he might be saying, "Hey, guys, *lighten up!*" If he can say this to us when we're fasting—by nature one of the most serious spiritual disciplines that exists—then what would he say to us about life in general?

From the Pulpit to the Pew

God astonished me one time as I prayed before I got up to preach: "You need to enjoy this."

Enjoy this? I thought of preaching as work, as labor, as an earnest endeavor. In fact, I had begun to question my use of humor—maybe it had grown out of place. After all, what could be more serious than talking about our eternal destiny? Did my use of humor undercut the content? I would far rather earn a reputation as a person who brings insight than as one who elicits chuckles.

Even so, laughter can often serve truth rather than oppose it. I say this because the way in which we view the pulpit (whether or not you actually preach behind one) gives a pretty accurate reflection of how we view the Christian life.

I once regularly met with a man under tremendous stress—the kind of stress that could send a weaker soul into a nervous breakdown. He had to endure a spiritual crisis, a relational crisis, and a vocational crisis—all at the same time. As we sat together one evening as part of the same small group, somebody told a hilarious story. Everyone started laughing until our sides hurt, which reminded someone else of an equally funny story. This went on for a good forty-five minutes until our diaphragms were sore from laughter.

"Well, this meeting got away from me," I thought. "We should have been praying for this guy all that time and giving him some counsel."

But as he stood up, he looked at us and said, "You have no idea how much this ministered to me tonight."

Ministered? With *laughter?* The truth is, he got exactly what he needed.

Earnest counsel and fervent prayer certainly have a place—but sometimes hurting people just need to laugh. Effective ministry recognizes what is most appropriate and when.

Let me be up front: if somebody relies on humor to cover up a lack of spiritual insight and studied wisdom, he or she has a sham "ministry." Laughter should illustrate, prepare for, and point to truth, not substitute for it. But when humor can serve Christ's cause —bringing people in, lightening their heavy loads, creating little mental "rests" for the next convicting point—it becomes God's servant.

After all, God created laughter. Why can't we celebrate him as we use what he created to help make his points? *It's a fact—I think a significant one—that humans are the only creatures who laugh.* Laughter, in this sense, gloriously reflects being made in God's image.

Surprised by the Humor of Christ

Some years ago, one of my favorite writers, Elton Trueblood, challenged me. He told of the time he was reading the Bible to his son in all seriousness when his boy started cracking up. The passage that his four-year-old found so funny? Jesus' comment about a man who had a plank in his eye and yet tried to remove a speck from someone else's eye (Matthew 7:3–5).

Trueblood's son considered this hilarious—sort of a Three

Stooges skit in the making. This experience opened up the esteemed philosopher-father to view the rest of Jesus' comments from an entirely new perspective. Trueblood writes:

> It is necessary, first, to do something to challenge the conventionalized picture of a Christ who never laughed.... There are numerous passages in the recorded teaching which are practically incomprehensible when regarded as sober prose, but which are luminous once we become liberated from the gratuitous assumption that Christ never joked. In some cases the recognition of humor is a genuine solvent.[2]

Trueblood goes on to warn that "a misguided piety has made us fear that acceptance of [Christ's] obvious wit and humor would somehow be mildly blasphemous or sacrilegious. Religion, we think, is serious business, and serious business is incompatible with banter."[3]

A thoughtful reading of Scripture, unencumbered by a false piety or sobriety, reveals Jesus' humor. For example, when Jesus asks if someone would put a lamp under a bushel or under a bed instead of putting it on a nightstand, his contemporaries would have laughed. Back then, a lamp didn't use a lightbulb for illumination. Any "lamp" involved an *open flame*. Now read it as his hearers would have understood it: If you had an open flame, would you "hide" it under a bushel of wheat? A straw-filled bed? Of course not! This is absurdity to the point of humor. If you read this in the context of the first century, you can hear the people laughing in response to Jesus' creative sarcasm.*

A fellow writer, Dave Moore, gave me this provocative quote from the great nineteenth-century Baptist preacher Charles Spurgeon, who apparently revered the power of laughter from the pulpit:

---

* In his book *The Humor of Christ*, Trueblood uses this passage as one example of Christ's humor.

I must confess that I would rather hear people laugh than I would see them asleep in the house of God; and I would rather get the truth into them through the medium of ridicule than I would have the truth neglected, or leave the people to perish through lack of reception of the truth. I do believe in my heart that there may be as much holiness in a laugh as in a cry; and that, sometimes, to laugh is the better thing of the two, for I may weep, and be murmuring, and repining [expressing discontent], and thinking all sorts of bitter thoughts about God; while, at another time, I may laugh the laugh of sarcasm against sin.... I do not know why ridicule is to be given up to Satan as a weapon to be used against us, and not to be employed by us as a weapon against him.[4]

Lighten Up

Despite Scripture's occasional use of humor, a certain element within the faith community still thinks that all "true" ministry must remain somber, or that the "holiest" people are also the most serious. Extreme and inappropriate levity *can* be a spiritual failing and a way to escape rather than confront life, but the absence of a sense of humor also poorly reflects on the image of God — who himself laughs and who created laughter.

Jesus' example should teach us to reject outright the wrongheaded notion that humor and seriousness are enemies rather than allies. You can make a very serious point with a very funny story. And funny moments often serve serious ministry.

In his marvelous book *Leadership from the Inside Out*, author Kevin Harney makes this observation:

I need to laugh more often. I sat with a woman whose husband, the man who said, "For better and for worse," ran off with a woman half his age. I cared, prayed, and felt helpless to relieve her deep pain. I battled through a board meeting with a gifted group of leaders who couldn't resolve a critical issue. I did a funeral for a seven-year-old boy whose body had been ravaged by leukemia. I processed ministry challenges with a volunteer who does not really fit where she is serving. Have you ever had to fire a volunteer? As the week comes to a close, I could really use a friend who will talk with me, laugh with me, go see a comedy with me. Sometimes I feel that if I can't laugh, I'll lose my mind. And some days laughter is hard to come by.[5]

Are you in a tough marriage or supporting someone else who's in one? Does your heart feel broken by a rebellious child? Does your boss, or the lack of a job, tempt you toward anxiety, worry, and stress? Are you a young person trying to find your way in this world but feeling all too alone and sometimes even lost? Has your heart shattered into a million pieces through disappointment after disappointment? Because we are humans, not gods, heavy responsibility devoid of laughter and pleasure can destroy us.[6] God has created a healing balm—laughter. Spiritually, it will lift us up and give us the strength to face life's serious challenges.

I once ran a marathon in the middle of June, and it was a "black balloon" day. Race organizers flew the black balloon to warn people of the heat and humidity index, telling runners to slow their pace and advising runners with health issues to consider dropping out.

I come from the Pacific Northwest and have lived for decades next to Bellingham Bay. A few times each year, the temperature may stretch to eighty degrees or more, but usually it pulls back into the seventies after about ninety minutes. We hear about humidity but rarely experience it firsthand—at least not in a suffocating way. In short, Duluth, Minnesota, was warmer and more humid at the 7:00 a.m. starting time than the middle of the afternoon ever gets in my backyard.

After thirteen miles at a decent pace, I knew trouble lay ahead. My body just wasn't used to this. The marathon collapsed into a pursuit of each water stop. Aid stations stood like oases about two miles apart from each other. Volunteers showered us with cold, wet sponges, ice cubes, and drinks. I forgot about the finish line and just focused on making it to the next aid station.

Think of laughter as an aid station during a hot marathon. Much work must take place between aid stations, but laughter gives us a mental, spiritual, emotional, and even physical break to face the challenge ahead. The more serious your situation, the more strenuous your work, the more you need to laugh. I've blown by aid stations during cool Seattle marathons and even at Boston; I didn't skip a single one in Duluth.

Shortly we'll get very practical about how to cultivate holy laughter, but before then, I need to make one important point.

Two Competing Forces

Many of us have difficulty embracing humor because our obedience to Scripture requires us to simultaneously adhere to two seemingly competing forces — sobriety and celebration.

The Gospels, after all, lead to the crucifixion of Jesus. When my wife and I went to the move theater to watch Mel Gibson's *The Passion of the Christ* and saw people walking in with tubs of popcorn and bags of M&M's, it made us wonder, "What did these people think they were going to see?"

Because the Gospels *do* carry heavy truths — the threat of damnation, the hope of salvation, the horrific price paid by Jesus on Calvary — it makes sense why we might read all of the Gospels backward, through the suffering of the cross. Theologically, to do so seems appropriate. The cross sheds light on all of Jesus' words.

Looked at another way, however, the fact that God poured out his wrath for our sin onto the body of his Son *is the very thing that makes laughter possible.* The ongoing feelings of sobriety and humility over the reality that our sin exacted such a high price lead to a corresponding celebration that God willingly made such a precious sacrifice, turning us from spiteful rebels into adopted and privileged sons and daughters of the kingdom. Jesus didn't die to make us miserable; *he died so that we could rise.*

We need to have large enough minds to hold seriousness, obligation, and responsibility in tension with enjoyment, laughter, and fun. The overly serious could blow me out of the water with a few choice quotes: Take up your cross *daily.* Be vigilant *always.* Be careful because your enemy the devil prowls around, looking for ways to tempt and destroy you.

These precious truths call for life-changing decisions. But they are not the *only* things that Jesus lived and said. Easter Sunday follows Good Friday. Jesus told his disciples to go away and get some rest. He provided wine for a wedding party — in a sufficiently emphatic fashion that we can assume Jesus wouldn't necessarily consider a sugary wedding punch "holier" than wine. He said that friends of the groom should celebrate and party while they still have the groom with them. Jesus heard himself called a glutton and a drunkard.

Fasting, experiencing conviction, dying to our own desires — these bedrock truths are not the only truths. God created us with the capacity to cry and also with the capacity to laugh. I want to worship him while doing *both.*

I love G. K. Chesterton's take on this: "I do not know why touching the heart should always be connected only with the idea of touching it to compassion or a sense of distress. The heart can be touched to joy and triumph; the heart can be touched to amusement."[7]

How can Christians laugh in the face of Good Friday? We do so because we read further along to Easter Sunday — and further yet to the "new heaven and the new earth," where God will wipe away every tear and usher us into pleasures forevermore (Revelation 21:1 – 4). Elton Trueblood writes, "Christianity fits man's deepest need because it makes him concentrate on joys which do not pass away, rather than on the inevitable grief which is superficial.... The well-known humor of the Christian is not a way of denying the tears, but rather a way of affirming something which is deeper than tears."[8]

Ultimately, it comes down to this: If Jesus used humor, then by definition *God* uses humor. And if *God* uses humor, then why can't his disciples? If Jesus thought he could make a particular point better understood and more easily received with a slight chuckle, how dare we shackle contemporary teachers of his truth to the somber, the overly serious, and the humorless? Sometimes as believers, and certainly as preachers, we *do* take ourselves too seriously.

Someone might counter: How can you take *preaching the gospel* too seriously? What could be more serious than *that*?

Here's how. In my arrogance, I assume my sermon is the most important point of that believer's life when, in fact, any sermon I utter is just one touch point — among many — that God uses to call this believer into maturity. Perhaps God first begins to open someone's eyes with a life event — something goes wrong, someone gets hurt, someone says something that alerts the believer she needs to grow in a particular area. God then challenges her by leading her to have a conversation with someone, perhaps over a cup of coffee, and God then builds on that with an insight she gains as she watches a play, reads a novel, or even watches a movie. God buttresses his case with a providentially placed Scripture in her devotional time and then may use my sermon as the exclamation point to bring the teaching home. I'm just a cog in the machine — perhaps an important cog, but even so, only one piece among many. Only arrogance can assume more than that.

It's healthy for us to laugh at ourselves, admit our limitations, and show that we all struggle with the truth that is greater than all of us. I take being an example very seriously—but my example must include how I handle and respond to my failures.

Maryland pastor C.J. Mahaney, who leads the Sovereign Grace churches, has often left me speechless following his compelling presentations of profound truth, while also helping me understand the absurdity and ridiculousness of our sinful rebellion. One time he seasoned a sermon with a hilarious anecdote of the time he launched into a disagreement with his wife at an expensive restaurant. His wife thought they could postpone the disagreement until a more appropriate time. C.J. had geared up for this discussion all day long and would not be denied.

Any experienced husband can guess what happened. The expensive "romantic" evening ended in utter ruin. C.J. spoke for all men when he recalled his personal thoughts after receiving the check for a miserable night out: "You idiot! The next time you pick a fight with your wife, do it at a Burger King!" It was healthy and holy to laugh at an ordinary, everyday example, seeing our own sin made fun of and mirrored in C.J.'s. That holy humor helped plant the teaching truth in my soul—giving it a much longer life than it would have enjoyed otherwise.

Growing Laughter

When pastors use appropriate humor in the pulpit, they model to their congregations how one can be "hilariously holy," which is another way of saying they model how to be hilariously *healthy*. Consider the compelling physical benefits of laughter, as summarized in a University of Maryland Medical Center study, which found that laughter benefits our cardiovascular system so much that it can be likened to exercise. Dr. Michael Miller, a lead researcher in the study, concluded:

> The magnitude of change we saw ... is similar to the benefit we might see with aerobic activity, but without the aches, pains, and muscle tensions associated with exercise.... We don't recommend that you laugh and not exercise, but we do recommend that you try to laugh on a regular basis. Thirty minutes of exercise three times a week, and fifteen minutes of laughter on a daily basis is probably good for the vascular system.[9]

Laughter has also been connected with reducing stress, lowering blood pressure, elevating mood, boosting the immune system, and, perhaps most important, fostering positive relationships, which makes us healthier in so many ways.

Shouldn't we intentionally grow something this powerful? How can we bring more holy laughter into our lives?

First, if you're single, put a good sense of humor near the top of your wish list for a future spouse. When I hear wives talk about their husbands, far more often than they ever mention their man's physical appearance, they'll say, "I love his sense of humor." Life is simply much more pleasant when you live with someone who makes you laugh. If you marry a dreary person, life may seem like one long drag. Physical attractiveness fades, while good humor constantly refines itself.

Second, if you're already married, you can still inject a good dose of humor into family life by embracing humility. We must learn to laugh at ourselves — not in a malicious sense, but in the sense that we recognize our silly mistakes and can laugh at them instead of cry about them. As we embrace God's forgiveness and the true love of others, we can become secure enough to admit we say and do dumb things. Because I know my family loves and respects me, when I do something *really* stupid, I can't wait to get home and tell everyone about it, and we'll all laugh together. If we take ourselves too seriously or feel threatened by a lack of love, we'll never have the atmosphere needed to laugh *with* each other instead of *at* each other. (Parents, please take care. A lot of kids get deeply wounded when they feel they're being laughed *at*.)

Third, pursue relationships with people who have a good sense of humor. Invite people into your home who lighten up the room, who love to tell stories, and who have that infectious kind of personality that tends to rub off on others. If your own family can't generate the laughter, invite others who can. Remember the reason a family we know used to regularly "borrow" our younger daughter, Kelsey, for their vacations? She brings fun wherever she goes.

Fourth, as much as preachers like to talk down Hollywood movies and television watching, find those few movies or TV shows that can make you laugh without shame. My son and I love *The Office.* Our daughter Allison prefers to join me when I watch reruns of the more relational *Mad about You.* I've found that I can even join my younger daughter when she watches *Gilmore Girls*, though I have to confess that my brain gets a little tired from its trademark rapid-fire dialogue. It's tough for me to make it through an entire episode. When my wife and I saw the movie *Dan in Real Life*, we laughed so hard we decided we needed to go see it again — and I'm sure we'll rent it in the future. The Internet has some hilarious and entirely appropriate humor sites.

Since humor is so personal, I hesitate to make any suggestions; but just a little searching will help you find a positive way to reach your "fifteen minutes a day" doctor's prescription.

For the more literary types, any number of novelists and memoir writers focus on humor — and some of them even deliver. I'm wary of bringing certain books and authors on an airplane, because I know I'm likely to disturb those around me by laughing out loud.

If someone you know is feeling down, find a good, funny card to lift them up. Let's say you and your spouse, or you and your roommate, seem to be butting heads about trivial stuff. Sometimes one good dose of laughter can break the tension. Do something fun together and thereby oil the squeaky joints of the relationship.

Your Glory

During an intense time of ministry transition, a very religious woman responded to a colleague's lighthearted comment with laughter, as did everyone in the room. She then tried to control herself, even saying out loud, "I bind the spirit of laughter."

I wanted to shout, "*Why?*"

It is our glory to laugh as God laughs, since he made us in his image. As part of our eternal destiny, secured in the finished work of Jesus Christ, it is our blessing to laugh. As servants of a reigning King who will set all things right, it is our privilege to laugh. Because we are adopted children of a generous Father, it is our birthright to laugh. The New Jerusalem Bible translates James 2:13 like this: "Mercy can afford to laugh at judgement."

We, beneficiaries of God's mercy, can *laugh*.

The only thing that this very religious woman should have bound was a haughty religious spirit.

Laugh, church, laugh — celebrating the goodness of God all the while.

DISCUSSION AND REFLECTION

1. Did you grow up in a faith tradition that embraced laughter or one that viewed it with suspicion? What do you think is the most biblical attitude toward laughter? What are the limits, if any?

2. Do you agree with Elton Trueblood that Jesus made significant use of humor in his own ministry? Support your belief with biblical examples. How should our discoveries in Scripture guide our own acceptance or wariness of the use of humor in church and social life?

3. Has there ever been a time in your life when laughter proved to be an effective medicine? Describe it.

4. Has there ever been a time in your life when you were hurt by laughter, or when you believed humor was used inappropriately — to hurt or to cover up a lack of commitment, insight, or compassion? Describe it.

5. How, practically, with our friends and family and when reaching out to others, can Christians balance the "two competing forces" Gary talks about — the seriousness and sobriety of the gospel message, along with a hilarious celebration of the same?

6. Do you need to cultivate more humor in your life, or do you believe you need the opposite — to take life more seriously? How will you achieve meeting your particular need?

EPILOGUE

It seemed like a dream, too good to be true,
  when GOD returned Zion's exiles.
We laughed, we sang,
  we couldn't believe our good fortune.
We were the talk of the nations —
  "GOD was wonderful to them!"
GOD was wonderful to us;
  we are one happy people.

Psalm 126:1–3 MSG

In the summer of 2008, Second Baptist Church in Houston invited my family to spend the entire month of August with them, preaching every Saturday, Sunday, and Wednesday.

I know — Houston, in *August*.

Even so, we had a marvelous month. I have the highest respect for Dr. Ed Young and his son, Ben, and for the incredible community God is building in Houston. Having my family with me just before two of our children headed out for college remains a highlight.

Because of the onset of school, however, my family left Houston two weeks before I did. When you know your family is breaking up because of life's realities — when you can literally count the months, then the weeks, then the days, and finally the hours before your family transforms from full to half empty — each day comes seasoned with a little desperation. I drank in every sweet moment, but in a slightly bitter sort of way.

The morning I dropped off my family at the airport, I got into a suddenly empty SUV and found it difficult to breathe. It would have scared and perhaps even appalled my wife to see the way I broke down. I don't remember ever crying so much, so long, or so painfully. Somehow I made it back to our condo. The place we had shared now held only memories. I walked into the rooms where the kids had stayed, sanctified by their presence. That day I ate lunch at a restaurant where Graham and I had shared a meal with Ben Young, wishing I could sit in the same booth we had occupied two weeks earlier. I went to the Starbucks where our family sat for a drink before we played laser tag. I saw a copy of a novel that my daughter had flipped through while we waited. I picked it up and held it, thinking, "Kelsey touched this." In a curious way, I didn't want to let it go.

I spent the rest of the day in a fog. I had to tweak my sermon for that weekend (when you're going to speak to more than twenty thousand people, you make sure you're prepared), but other than that, I was a wreck. Thank God for the Olympics, which helped me stop thinking continually about my ache, my loss.

The next morning I woke up early, prepared a cup of tea, and sat down with my Bible. I thought of the many great pleasures my family had enjoyed together: diamond-level seats at a major league baseball game, an amazing lunch at the Taste of Texas Restaurant (highly recommended), fun times at a Galveston Island water park, Graham and Ben surfing early in the morning while I ran along the beach—just being together, laughing and praying and talking— all noble pleasures, all good gifts from God. Their intensity made their cessation all the more painful.

As I prayed, however, it dawned on me that because of Jesus Christ, I will never feel the pain of separation from God as I have

felt the pain of separation from my family. There will never be a
moment when God leaves, when I have to "say good-bye" to my
Savior. Even the best pleasures in this world are transitory and vulnerable. We shouldn't despise them or discount them because of
that, but it does mean we deserve the name "fool" if we set the
foundations of our life and joy on them.

Using pleasure to point us back to God instead of allowing it
to compete with him (or worse, letting it draw us away from him)
roots us in the greatest pleasure that will never, *ever* end.

God has given me many pleasures in my lifetime of pursuing
him. If it were all to end today, I could only say, "What a ride, Lord
—what an amazing ride!" He has sustained me with the pleasures
of family, vocation, and worship, and he has seasoned these profound joys with the smaller delights of drinking a well-made cup
of chai tea, reading another brilliant novel by a favorite writer, running on an autumn afternoon, and laughing with friends.

I have no problem believing that God may have granted me
unusual pleasures, knowing I have such a weak, vulnerable soul.
Friends of mine have faced life challenges and even catastrophes
that overwhelm me just thinking about them. Perhaps God knew
I'd crumble in the face of such trial. All we can do is walk the road
God lays out for us.

Even so, those who are wise find their supreme pleasure in God.
Earth's best pleasures are all transitory; they all seem to end almost
as soon as they begin. But as tools that point us to our ultimate joy,
they can become very effective friends.

I pray earnestly that when you set down this book, you will
revel in the many pleasures God has granted you. Thank him for
these pleasures, and let your satisfied soul draw others to the Christ
you've learned to enjoy above all else.

ACKNOWLEDGMENTS

I want to thank several early readers who provided comments on initial drafts and chapters: Mark Grambo, Jerry Thomas, Mary Kay Smith, Dr. Rebecca Wilke, Lisa Thomas, Bryan Halferty, Kevin Harney, and Dr. Melody Rhode. Merely mentioning your names does not do justice to the sacrifice of your time and talents on my behalf, but I am deeply grateful nonetheless. Any ministry this book represents was shaped considerably by your efforts and early comments.

I am also indebted to Dr. J. I. Packer, who graciously agreed to meet me halfway through the writing process, allowed me to present my thesis and thoughts in verbal form, and then gave me the confidence to pursue a direction I might otherwise have shied away from. Of course, any conclusions you read are mine alone, and none of the above people should be tainted by them.

Thanks are also due my agent, Curtis Yates, who has truly become a partner in this ministry; my assistant, Laura Thompson; and the editorial team at Zondervan, John Sloan and Dirk Buursma, who have been a joy to work with for a full decade now.

The marketing/publishing team at Zondervan has provided great support: Mike Salisbury, Tom Dean, Dudley Delffs, Steve Sammons, and John Raymond. I also owe a debt of gratitude to Scott Bolinder, who believed in (and invested in) this project when it was just an idea, and Moe Girkins, who stood behind it as it was launched.

NOTES

Chapter 1: THE TYRANNY OF TORRENTIAL THIRST

1. Thomas Chalmers, "The Expulsive Power of a New Affection," in *The Protestant Pulpit*, comp. Andrew Blackwood, (1947; repr., Grand Rapids: Baker, 1977), 50.
2. G. K. Chesterton, *Heretics* (1905; repr., Nashville: Nelson, 2000), 10.
3. Jürgen Moltmann, *Theology and Joy* (London: SCM Press, 1973), 52.
4. Chalmers, "Expulsive Power," 52.

Chapter 2: FORTIFYING OURSELVES WITH PLEASURE

1. Harper Lee, *To Kill a Mockingbird* (1960; repr., New York: HarperCollins, 1999), 49.
2. William Banowksy, *It's a Playboy World* (Old Tappan, N.J.: Spire, 1973), 117.
3. Karen Horney, *Neurosis and Human Growth* (1950; repr., New York: Norton, 1991), 141–42. I know I try some of my readers' patience by quoting rather widely, and Karen Horney (1885–1952) is one who may raise eyebrows. She was a famous German psychologist and initially started out as a disciple of Sigmund Freud until she broke with him over some significant issues. Please keep in mind that when I quote an author, I am not endorsing all that he or she has written; *I am using one particular quote to make one particular point.*
4. D. A. Carson, *Basics for Believers: An Exposition of Philippians* (Grand Rapids: Baker, 1996), 116.
5. Julian of Norwich, *Revelations of Divine Love*, trans. Elizabeth Spearing (New York: Penguin, 1998), 166–67.

Chapter 3: HOW OUR PLEASURE PLEASES GOD

1. Julian of Norwich, *Revelations of Divine Love*, trans. Elizabeth Spearing (New York: Penguin, 1998), 75.
2. John Lennon, "Whatever Gets You thru the Night," from *Walls and Bridges* (Apple Records, released October 1974).

3. Charles Francis Adams, *Familiar Letters of John Adams and His Wife Abigail Adams* (1875; repr., New York: Kessinger, 2007), 411.
4. François Fénelon, *Christian Perfection* (Minneapolis: Bethany House, 1975), 80.
5. Ibid.

Chapter 4: THE EARTH IS NOT THE WORLD

1. Karen Horney, *Neurosis and Human Growth* (1950; repr., New York: Norton, 1991), 117.
2. Frederik Buytendijk, "Les différences essentielles des fonctions psychiques de l'homme et des animaux," in *Vue sur la psychologie animale* (Paris: Vrin, 1930), 76; quoted in Elemér Hankiss, *Fear and Symbols* (Budapest: CEU Press, 2001), 219.
3. Shauna Niequist, *Cold Tangerines: Celebrating the Extraordinary Nature of Everyday Life* (Grand Rapids: Zondervan, 2007), 84.
4. Sam Storms, *Pleasures Evermore: The Life-Changing Power of Enjoying God* (Colorado Springs: NavPress, 2000), 162.
5. See John 2:1 – 10; Matthew 6:25 – 34; Matthew 9:14 – 15; John 11:33 – 44.
6. Quoted in John Brant, *Duel in the Sun: Alberto Salazar, Dick Beardsley, and America's Greatest Marathon* (New York: Rodale, 2006), 150.

Chapter 5: PARTY LIKE IT'S BIBLICAL TIME

1. Jürgen Moltmann, *Theology and Joy* (London: SCM Press, 1973), 45.
2. Ibid., 53.
3. John Calvin, *Calvin's Commentaries: Philippians, Colossians, and Thessalonians* (Grand Rapids: Baker, 2003), 200.
4. F. F. Bruce, *The Epistles to the Colossians, to Philemon, and to the Ephesians* (New International Commentary on the New Testament; Grand Rapids: Eerdmans, 1984), 253.
5. Randy Alcorn, *Heaven* (Wheaton, Ill.: Tyndale, 2004), 297 – 98; 373 – 90. Randy's comments about Christoplatonism are sprinkled throughout the book. Appendix A includes a helpful section that addresses the assumptions of Christoplatonism more fully.
6. Henry Drummond, *The Greatest Thing in the World: and 21 Other Addresses* (London: Collins, 1953), 82.
7. Ibid., 83 – 84.
8. C. S. Lewis, *The Screwtape Letters* (New York: Macmillan, 1951), 49.
9. Ibid., 112.

Chapter 6: PRACTICAL PLEASURE

1. Douglas Weiss tells this story in his book *The Power of Pleasure* (Carlsbad, Calif.: Hay House, 2007), 127–29.
2. Ibid., 87.
3. Shauna Niequist, *Cold Tangerines: Celebrating the Extraordinary Nature of Everyday Life* (Grand Rapids: Zondervan, 2007), 106.
4. François Fénelon, *Christian Perfection* (Minneapolis: Bethany House, 1975), 21.
5. Weiss, *Power of Pleasure*, 176–77.
6. Elton Trueblood, *The Company of the Committed* (New York: Harper, 1961), 43.
7. Fénelon, *Christian Perfection*, 141.
8. I'm indebted to Dr. James Houston for this analogy; see his book *In Pursuit of Happiness: Finding Genuine Fulfillment in Life* (Colorado Springs: NavPress, 1996), 238.
9. Ibid., 249.

Chapter 7: WHAT'S YOUR PLEASURE?

1. Douglas Weiss, *The Power of Pleasure* (Carlsbad, Calif.: Hay House, 2007), 16.
2. Ibid., 16.
3. David Powlison, "Innocent Pleasures," *Journal of Biblical Counseling* 23 (Fall 2005): 32.

Chapter 8: SPIRITUAL FERNS

1. Karen Horney, *Neurosis and Human Growth* (1950; repr., New York: Norton, 1991), 65.
2. Ibid., 6.
3. Patrick Carnes, *Don't Call It Love* (New York: Bantam, 1991), 279.
4. François Fénelon, *Christian Perfection* (Minneapolis: Bethany House, 1975), 20–21.
5. A. J. Russell, *For Sinners Only* (London: Hodder & Stoughton, 1932), 291.
6. James Houston, *In Pursuit of Happiness: Finding Genuine Fulfillment in Life* (Colorado Springs: NavPress, 1996), 41, emphasis added.

Chapter 9: PRESERVING PLEASURE

1. Sam Storms, *Pleasures Evermore* (Colorado Springs: NavPress, 2000), 145.
2. Douglas Weiss, *The Power of Pleasure* (Carlsbad, Calif.: Hay House, 2007), 52.
3. Ibid., 53.
4. Ibid.
5. Heather Louise Earnshaw, "An Ethic of Enjoyment" (master's thesis, Regent College, December 1990), 69.

6. James Houston, *In Pursuit of Happiness; Finding Genuine Fulfillment in Life* (Colorado Springs: NavPress, 1996), 47.

7. William Shakespeare, "Sonnet 94," in *The Works of Shakespeare* (New York: Routledge, 1864), 774.

Chapter 10: DANGEROUS PLEASURES

1. Tony Kornheiser, *I'm Back for More Cash* (New York: Villard, 2002), 250–51.

2. Ibid., 251.

3. François Fénelon, *Christian Perfection* (Minneapolis: Bethany House, 1975), 7.

4. All quotations here (and in the next paragraph) are taken from Steven Reinberg, "Drink a Little, Stay Active, Save Your Heart," January 9, 2008, MyHeartCentral.com: *www.healthcentral.com/heart-disease/news-199348 -31.html* (February 24, 2009).

5. "Heart Attack and Acute Coronary Syndrome," Walgreens Health Library: *www.walgreens.com/library/contents.html?docid=000012&doctype=10* (February 24, 2009).

6. Mark Driscoll, *The Radical Reformission: Reaching Out without Selling Out* (Grand Rapids: Zondervan, 2004), 146.

7. G. K. Chesterton, *Heretics* (1905; repr., Nashville: Nelson, 2000), 52.

8. David Powlison, "Innocent Pleasures," *Journal of Biblical Counseling* 23 (Fall 2005): 25.

9. Ibid., 25.

10. Ibid., 21.

11. Ibid., 23.

Chapter 11: THE COST OF PLEASURE

1. John Calvin, *Institutes of the Christian Religion*, ed. John T. McNeill (1559; repr., Philadelphia: Westminster, 1960), 1:839.

Chapter 12: FAMILY PLEASURE

1. Jean Vanier, *Becoming Human* (New York: Paulist, 1998), 21.

2. Ibid., 26.

3. Ibid.

4. David Powlison, "Innocent Pleasures," *Journal of Biblical Counseling* 23 (Fall 2005): 34.

Chapter 13: SINGING IN EXILE

1. Zlata Filipović, *Zlata's Diary* (New York: Viking, 1994), 66.

2. Clarence Thomas, *My Grandfather's Son: A Memoir* (New York: HarperCollins, 2007), 129.

3. John Piper, *Future Grace* (Sisters, Ore.: Multnomah, 1995), 386.

4. Tricia Rhodes, *Sacred Chaos: Spiritual Disciplines for the Life You Have* (Downers Grove, Ill.: InterVarsity, 2008); Kay Warren, *Dangerous Surrender: What Happens When You Say Yes to God* (Grand Rapids: Zondervan, 2007).

5. Kim Painter, "Life's Little Pleasures Can Relieve Illness, Stress," *USA Today*, May 11, 2008, D4.

6. Julian of Norwich, *Revelations of Divine Love*, trans. Elizabeth Spearing (New York: Penguin, 1998), 69.

7. See C. S. Lewis, *The Weight of Glory* (1949; repr., New York: HarperCollins, 2001).

8. Jacques Ellul, *Hope in Time of Abandonment* (New York: Seabury, 1973), 201.

Chapter 14: HILARIOUSLY HOLY

1. Quoted in Bert Ghezzi, *Mystics and Miracles: True Stories of Lives Touched by God* (Chicago: Loyola, 2004), 124.

2. Elton Trueblood, *The Humor of Christ* (New York: Harper & Row, 1964), 10.

3. Ibid., 15.

4. Charles Spurgeon, *Lectures to My Students* (Grand Rapids: Zondervan, 1954), 389. Dave Moore includes this quote in his *The Last Men's Book You'll Ever Need: What the Bible Says about Guy Stuff* (Nashville: Broadman & Holman, 2008), 3–4.

5. Kevin Harney, *Leadership from the Inside Out: Examining the Inner Life of a Healthy Church Leader* (Grand Rapids: Zondervan, 2007), 135.

6. I credit Jürgen Moltmann (*Theology and Joy* [London: SCM Press, 1973], 46) for inspiring this thought. His exact words border on being too academic for this type of book, so I paraphrased the thought. Here's his original: "Infinite responsibility destroys a human being because he is only man and not god. I have an idea that laughter is able to mediate between the infinite magnitude of our tasks and the limitations of our strength."

7. G. K. Chesterton, *Heretics* (1905; repr., Nashville: Nelson, 2000), 109.

8. Trueblood, *Humor of Christ*, 30, 32.

9. "University of Maryland School of Medicine Study Shows Laughter Helps Blood Vessels Function Better," University of Maryland Medical Center press release, March 7, 2005, *www.umm.edu/news/releases/laughter2.htm* (February 24, 2009).

ONLINE VIDEO
SMALL GROUP DISCUSSION
QUESTIONS

Please go to *www.zondervan.com/purepleasure*
to purchase the six *Pure Pleasure* online video sessions.

INTRODUCTION

Getting together in a small group to study the material found in *Pure Pleasure* is one of the best ways to make it stick—and to have a lot of fun in the process. To that end, we have developed a six-session online video curriculum featuring the teaching of Gary Thomas to get the most out of the journey you are undertaking to capture (or recapture) pure pleasure in your life.

Before your group meeting, it would be helpful for you to read (or reread) the chapters in *Pure Pleasure* associated with the session, but this is not required. These times of discussion do not rely on whether or not you've read the chapter in advance. The purpose is to enjoy the interaction and to learn from it. You can always reread the chapters later, if you wish.

What Materials Are Needed for a Successful Small Group?

- Computer, DVD, or other device with the six downloaded video teaching sessions by author Gary Thomas
- *Pure Pleasure* book by Gary Thomas (curriculum discussion questions at the back of the book
- Bible — Old and New Testaments (one per group member)
- Pen or pencil for everyone
- Watch or clock with which to monitor time

Good to Know

This curriculum can work equally well in church and home groups. Each of the six sessions is planned for approximately 55 minutes in length between the beginning of the viewing of the video and the conclusion of the discussion time together. Feel free to adapt each session to your particular group. Reword or add questions if you wish. If you sense that a certain question reaches beyond your comfort zone, you may simply omit it, or at least recognize that not everyone needs to answer every question. On the other hand, don't be afraid to tackle tough topics. You may not come up with all the answers, or even reach agreement among yourselves — and that's OK. Above all, approach these sessions with an expectant spirit. For further insights, please read and recommend to your group Gary Thomas's *Pure Pleasure*, the book on which this curriculum is based.

Session 1: PLEASURE:
A GOOD, GOD-GIVEN THING

This session is based on chapters 1, 2, and 3 in Pure Pleasure.

1. What has been your attitude toward pleasure in the past? How has your upbringing influenced this attitude — positively or negatively?

2. Do you believe that you've been biblically informed about pleasure or that you're just reacting to feelings, guilt twinges, or life experiences? How has this session helped you to look at pleasure in a more biblical light?

3. Have you ever known someone who had a very healthy, biblical attitude toward pleasure? What were they like? What did you learn from them?

4. Have you ever known someone who had a very unhealthy attitude toward pleasure? Where did they fall short, and what did it look like?

5. How does understanding how your pleasure brings pleasure to God encourage you and other believers to accept pleasure in an appropriate context?

Session 2: ENJOYING THE EARTH WITHOUT LOVING THE WORLD

This session is based on chapters 4 and 5 in Pure Pleasure.

1. Which image do you believe most Christians adhere to — viewing the world as a prostitute (a place of temptation) or as a mother (nurturing our faith and worship)?

2. Read Deuteronomy 8:7 – 19. What does this passage teach you about how to enjoy the earth without falling in love with the world?

3. How can learning to enjoy earth's pleasures fire up your worship?

4. Describe a time when you felt vividly alive to the world in a positive, healthy sense. What were you doing? What spiritual lessons can you draw from this encounter?

5. Read Colossians 2:20 – 23. What is the danger of always going "one step further" to avoid sin? What would be a more appropriate guide?

Session 3: SPIRITUAL FERNS

This session is based on chapter 8 in Pure Pleasure.

1. Why do you think Christians so often fall into the trap of thinking they are the "exception," and run themselves into the ground or into an unhealthy lifestyle?

2. Gary mentions tiredness, loneliness, and serving without joy as three major spiritual ferns. Which one are you most likely to fall prey to?

3. What are some other "spiritual ferns" that Gary doesn't mention?

4. In what ways can you as a Christian keep watch over each other to help your well-intentioned brothers and sisters see when they may be drifting into unhealthy lifestyles?

5. Discuss several lifestyle changes you can commit to make in the coming days and weeks to overcome your personal spiritual fern(s).

Session 4: THE COST OF PLEASURE

This session is based on chapter 11 in Pure Pleasure.

1. Read Deuteronomy 14:22–29 and 1 Kings 8:65–66. What do you think these Old Testament passages teach Christians about the legitimacy of celebrating God's goodness, sometimes even in extravagant ways?

2. Read Luke 14:12–14. What does Jesus' teaching add to the Old Testament notion of enjoying God's goodness?

3. With worldwide media coverage today of frequent natural disasters, famines, and the like, and global missionary endeavors always in need of additional funds, how can Christians find a balance between sacrificial giving to charity and God's kingdom work and appropriate times of celebration and personal pleasure?

4. In what way are you most likely to spend money on pleasure — frequent small purchases or occasional large ones? What are the cautions that Christians should be mindful of in both instances?

5. After viewing this video, reading the passages, and engaging in this discussion, how would you evaluate the appropriateness of your spending in areas that could be labeled personal pleasures? Where do you need to grow? What changes do you need to make?

Session 5: FAMILY PLEASURE:
BECOMING A SERVANT OF THEIR JOY

This session is based on chapter 12 in Pure Pleasure.

1. Did (or does) your family of origin regularly play together? How so?

2. What do you think are some of the causes behind married couples drifting into "utilitarian" relationships that are short on enjoyment and long on responsibility? What can couples do to guard against this drift?

3. How can having fun together serve the parent/child relationship? Why do you think this is often seen as particularly difficult during the teen years?

4. How do you think children of various ages can become servants of their parents' joy? How might learning how to do this foster a child's own spiritual growth and preparation for adulthood?

5. How can the experience of a parent becoming a servant of their child's joy repair a strained relationship? How can this accent on serving your child's joy be balanced with a need to maintain authority, set boundaries, and hold him or her accountable?

6. List one or two ways you can worship God by bringing pleasure to a family member in the coming days or weeks.

Session 6: THE POWER OF PLEASURE TO HELP US ENDURE DIFFICULT TIMES

This session is based on chapter 13 in Pure Pleasure.

1. Describe one of the most difficult periods of your life. What role, if any, did pleasure have in helping you get through this season? In what ways might a greater consciousness of the need for pleasure have helped you to have done even better?

2. How can a commitment to marshaling the power of pleasure help:

   • an office that is under enormous stress?
   • a church staff facing serious issues?
   • a family in which one member has a serious medical issue?
   • a student who feels overwhelmed with life?

3. What do you think are some of the dangers for someone encountering an unsatisfying marriage, a frustrating employment (or unemployment) situation, a medical infirmity, or some other difficulty to try to "just get by" without thinking constructively about cultivating appropriate times of pleasure?

4. If God were to close the door to receiving pleasure in one area of your life (health, a relationship, vocation, etc.), how could you let go of bitterness and embrace the pleasures that are offered in other areas? What are some guidelines for making sure the "substitute" pleasures are healthy ones?

5. How can the spiritual pleasure of being in a personal relationship with God sustain you when other pleasures seem to be out of reach? Should you still seek other earthly pleasures? How so?

6. Think of someone you know who learned to cultivate a simple pleasure during a difficult season in their life. What can you learn from their example? Can you come up with examples of people who didn't cultivate pleasure and suffered accordingly? What might these examples teach you?

GARY THOMAS

Feel free to contact Gary. Though he cannot respond personally to all correspondence, he would love to get your feedback. (Please understand, however, that he is neither qualified nor able to provide counsel via email):

Gary Thomas
P.O. Box 29417
Bellingham, WA 98228-1417
GLT3@aol.com

For information about Gary's speaking schedule, visit his website (www.garythomas.com). To inquire about inviting Gary to your church, please write or call the Center for Evangelical Spirituality at 360-676-7773, or email his assistant: Laura@garythomas.com.

The Center for Evangelical Spirituality (CFES) is a ministry dedicated to fostering spiritual growth within the Christian community through an integrated study of Scripture, church history, and the Christian classics. We believe evangelical Christians can learn a great deal from historic Christian traditions without compromising the essential tenets of what it means to be an evangelical Christian. Accepting Scripture as our final and absolute authority, we seek to promote Christian growth and the refinement of an authentic Christian spirituality.

Sacred Pathways

Discover Your Soul's Path to God

Gary Thomas, Bestselling Author of Sacred Marriage

"Thou shalt not covet thy neighbor's spiritual walk." After all, it's his, not yours. Better to discover the path God designed *you* to take—a path marked by growth and fulfillment, based on your own unique temperament.

In *Sacred Pathways*, Gary Thomas strips away the frustration of a one-size-fits-all spirituality and guides you toward a path of worship that frees you to be you. If your devotional times have hit a snag, perhaps it's because you're trying to follow someone else's path.

This book unpacks nine distinct spiritual temperaments—their traits, strengths, and pitfalls. In one or more of them, you will see yourself and the ways you most naturally express your relationship with Jesus Christ. Whatever temperament or blend of temperaments best describes you, rest assured it's not by accident. It's by the design of a Creator who knew what he was doing when he made you according to his own unique specifications. *Sacred Pathways* will reveal the route you were made to travel, marked by growth and filled with the riches of a close walk with God.

Softcover: 978-0-310-24284-0

Pick up a copy today at your favorite bookstore!

Sacred Marriage

What If God Designed Marriage to Make Us Holy More Than to Make Us Happy?

Gary Thomas

Your marriage is more than a sacred covenant with another person. It is a spiritual discipline designed to help you know God better, trust him more fully, and love him more deeply.

Scores of books have been written that offer guidance for building the marriage of your dreams. But what if God's primary intent for your marriage isn't to make you happy — but holy? And what if your relationship isn't as much about you and your spouse as it is about you and God?

Everything about your marriage is filled with prophetic potential, with the capacity for discovering and revealing Christ's character. The respect you accord your partner; the forgiveness you humbly seek and graciously extend; the ecstasy, awe, and sheer fun of lovemaking; the history you and your spouse build with each other — in these and other facets of your marriage, *Sacred Marriage* uncovers the mystery of God's overarching purpose.

This book may well alter profoundly the contours of your marriage. It will most certainly change you. Because whether it is delightful or difficult, your marriage can become a doorway to a closer walk with God and to a spiritual integrity that, like salt, seasons the world around you with the savor of Christ.

Softcover: 978-0-310-24282-6

Pick up a copy today at your favorite bookstore!

ZONDERVAN®
.com

Authentic Faith

What If Life Isn't Meant to Be Perfect, but We Are Meant to Trust the One Who Is?

Gary Thomas, Bestselling Author of Sacred Marriage

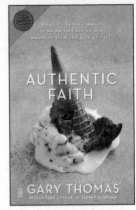

What if the spiritual disciplines that bring us closer to God are not the ones we control? Bestselling author Gary Thomas reveals the rich benefits that derive from embracing the harder truths of Scripture. With penetrating insight from Scripture and the Christian classics, along with colorful and engaging stories, Thomas's eye-opening look into what it means to be a true disciple of Jesus will encourage you, bolster your faith, and help you rise above shallow attachments to fix your heart on things of eternal worth.

Thomas shows us that authentic faith penetrates the most unlikely places. It is found when we die to ourselves and put others first. It is nurtured when we cultivate contentment instead of spending our energy trying to improve our lot in life. It is strengthened in suffering, persecution, waiting, and even mourning. Instead of holding on to grudges, authentic faith chooses forgiveness. And it lives with another world in mind, recognizing that what we do in this broken world will be judged.

Softcover: 978-0-310-25419-5

Pick up a copy today at your favorite bookstore!

Holy Available

What If Holiness Is about More Than What We Don't Do?

Gary Thomas, Bestselling author of Sacred Marriage

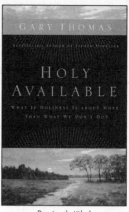

Previously titled
The Beautiful Fight

True Christian faith is a profoundly transformational experience in which every part of our being is marked by God's change and energized by his presence. This transformation takes us far beyond mere sin avoidance to a robust, "full-bodied" holiness in which we make ourselves "holy available" to God every minute of the day. From Starbucks, to the office, to the soccer fields, to the boardroom, believers have the opportunity to carry the presence of Christ wherever they go.

God offers the reader more than mere forgiveness; he wants to radically change and fill them with his presence, so they can experience an entirely different kind of life based not just on what they do or don't do but on who they are.

Yet while many Christians today profess belief, their Christianity has no pulse. Previously titled *The Beautiful Fight*, *Holy Available* is a manifesto of fully alive faith. Gary Thomas issues a compelling call for readers to see with Christ's eyes, feel with Christ's heart, and serve with Christ's hands. We make ourselves available to become "God oases," places of spiritual refuge where God can bring the hurting and lost to enjoy his presence and ministry.

Softcover: 978-0-310-29200-5

Pick up a copy today at your favorite bookstore!

ZONDERVAN®
.com